IN THE LAND OF
APHRODITE

IN THE LAND OF
APHRODITE

Libby Rowan-Moorhouse

Illustrated by the author

Libby Rowan - Moorhouse

Book Guild Publishing
Sussex, England

First published in Great Britain in 2005 by
The Book Guild Ltd
25 High Street
Lewes, East Sussex
BN7 2LU

Typesetting in Garamond by
Keyboard Services, Luton, Bedfordshire

Printed in Great Britain by
Antony Rowe Ltd, Chippenham, Wiltshire

A catalogue record for this book is available from
The British Library

ISBN 1 85776 923 6

*To the people of the village,
with affection*

Acknowledgements

I would like to thank Soteris Georgallis, of the London Cyprus High Commission, for his advice and help.

I would also like to thank Jan Chapman, whose endless patience and skill helped us both to get this story onto her word processor.

Once upon a time, there was a village. We lived there not long ago. How can I conjure up that other village now, in all this soft English rain, which is smudging my view of the old stone church opposite my window? Its yellow stones seem to be sinking even further into their bed of green mud as the relentless rain continues. Cars go past my window, sometimes their tyres going *whoosh! whoosh!* on the wet tarmac. The Potterton boiler hums all day long in my kitchen but, even in my sheepskin boots, my toes are as cold as the stones of St Mary's over the way.

How sharp and tangible are the memories of that other place! Close the eyes and the warm sun is back again, like the wasps in the grapevine. The heady smell is there, the smell of over-ripened grapes, which, as they fall, I must sweep from the roof terrace. Village sounds penetrate the heavy air: the frustrated braying of Madonna in her field, Old Demetri's hens scuffling in the orchard and ignoring the strident wooing of the bossy rooster, the women's ceaseless chatter as they sit outdoors with their stitching.

The problem in that other village was, of course, water. Never ever enough of it! The village priest, Father S., prayed for rain. We women, sitting at the back (we knew our place), prayed with him. The church was the property of the Virgin Mary, as is the one opposite, but it went by the Greek name of Ayios Maria. In winter time its doors were shut to keep in the fug from a number of gas heaters and from the votive candles and the incense. For most of the year, however, the doors stood open and the electric fans hummed above our heads. The voices of priest and chanters (male, of course, but for one twelve-year-old girl permitted to sing on special occasions) rang throughout the village with the help of loudspeakers. Summoned by bells, we watched the seasons come and go. We villagers lived much of our lives in the open air. People would say ours was a small paradise.

*   *   *

1

These days all news seems bad. Today the BBC announcer has dealt with the usual things – Tony Blair's problems with our National Health Service (or National Ill-Health Service, as one wit put it), our failing railways, our under-performing state schools etc. All that sort of thing. Next we moved on to our daily dose of the increasing problems with Iraq, bombs in Baghdad and the Bush and Blair headaches appertaining thereto. However, the next announcement came like a bolt from the blue. Why did the BBC announcer keep a tone as impassive as before, when what he had to say riveted me to the spot? (My actual spot was by the ironing board in my small kitchen, my flannelette nightie half pressed, the soft English rain falling silently outside.)

'Our correspondent reports from Nicosia,' said the voice, 'that the people of Cyprus, both in the north and south, are soon to vote in elections sponsored by the United Nations. The outcome of these elections will decide their future as citizens of a united Cyprus or whether the island remains divided, as it has done since 1974...'

A united Cyprus! I take a gulp of half stale coffee. The voice goes on:

'However, the move is expected to be opposed by Mr Rauf Denktash, the Turkish Cypriot leader of the Nationalist Party in the north...'

Good old Denktash! Still acting as a metaphorical fly in the ointment! He must be well into his late seventies by now, but advancing years have not dimmed his hearty distrust of all things Greek. This also applies to some of the Greek Cypriots themselves, those who fled to the south. Wounds stay fresh. Memories die hard. But here we are now, with the year 2004 advancing upon us and the dream of a united island within the grasp of all who wish her well, this ancient and lovely island with its turbulent past, but never before divided as now.

I make myself a fresh cup of coffee and take it into my small front room and, with the ironing piling up elsewhere, I allow my thoughts to float luxuriously backwards...

Tim and I arrived on the island in July 1997, exactly thirty-three years after the Turkish invasion of the north. As 'foreigners', of course, it had taken us time to appreciate quite how devastating for the local people this invasion and its consequences had been. Mass migrations of Greek Cypriots from the north and Turkish Cypriots from the south had followed, many even emigrating abroad, never to return. But in 'our' half of Nicosia, the Greek Cypriot half, we luxuriated for some weeks in the Hilton Hotel, barely aware of the privations that the people in the north were now still undergoing, or the sense of grievance nursed by all Cypriots alike.

In those early weeks in Nicosia I began to keep a somewhat erratic diary, a habit which I tried to keep up as time went by.

On 11th July I had written:

From our bedroom on the sixth floor of our hotel we can see to the north on the distant, dusty hills, two giant-sized crescents carved into the red earth. These symbols, we are told, are Turkey's reminder to their Greek Cypriot neighbours that this island is divided and, as far as one can see, will remain so. A United Nations buffer zone cuts this city in half, the no-go area patrolled by young men in blue berets with rifles and bored expressions. A number of young Greeks have attempted a crossing illegally and been martyred by the Turks for their pains. The Greek Cypriot must have a very good reason for crossing this zone; a once-yearly visit to an Orthodox church, perhaps, while his Turkish Cypriot counterpart may pay a similar visit to the Hala Sultan Tekke mosque in Larnaca. Even we foreigners, should we wish to cross, must leave our passports with the Turkish authorities and hurry home by sunset.

Greek Nicosia is a disappointment. Apart from the remains of the old Venetian walls, little of real archaeological interest for the hopeful visitor remains. While Tim has been meeting colleagues to do with his new job here, I took myself off yesterday to the archaeological museum, where tantalizing glimpses of the island's turbulent past stand about on plinths and in glass cabinets. In the mid–1870s the American Consul to Cyprus, by the name of Luigi di Cessnola, who rather fancied himself as a budding archaeologist, removed many antiquities from the island and sold some four thousand objects to the Metropolitan Museum of Art in New York. Here many Cypriot works of art are displayed, as they are also in the great museums in Boston, London and Paris. In the streets of Greek Nicosia modern progress is represented by the usual uninspired buildings, choking motor traffic and young girls drifting down pavements in tight trousers. Not for them the black stockings and headscarves worn by their grandmothers.

In early August I wrote to my mother in Australia:

At last I'm achieving a life's ambition to live in a village! Yes, we have found it! Forget about city life and all the rest of it. Tim says he is keen to give it a go as well, though his sincerity is a little suspect. Anything to keep me happy is his motto, but then he will have the stimulation of his work, whereas my days must be filled somehow and this could be 'it'. I will keep a diary and do some painting.

Our village (you can see I have already moved in in spirit, if not in fact, as Thekla says the house won't be ready until next week) is a kind of poor relation of the bigger village up the hill. We will be about two thousand feet above sea level, in the foothills of the Troodos, the mountains that sprawl over a huge chunk of our Greek part of the island.

It was such luck we found the house as, once we'd picked our two villages (either 'upper' or 'lower'), we became increasingly gloomy about the mounting list of places that some enthusiastic local would hurry us over to see. '*Ella, ella* [Come, come]. Yes, the aunt of my cousin has a nice house. I will show you,' or 'Demetrius, his sister she lives in New York. You know Demetrius? The husband of his sister, he has a very nice place. To sell? Yes, or to rent. Yes of course. *Ella.*' So we would follow, first tripping along with beating hearts, then following after with heavy tread, up one cobbled lane and down another, through a tumbledown archway, into a tumbledown house, through it and out again and across a tumbledown courtyard, through doors creaking on one hinge or none at all. Then behold! The house of the aunt of my cousin! There it stands, one part of it sliding downhill, the other part sliding up, with rectangular holes for windows, a first-floor balcony about to detach itself and crash into the weed-strewn garden, and a flight of stone steps leading up to it, that is also in a state of terminal decay which no amount of filler can disguise. Both villages are full of such houses, many of the owners having fled over twenty years ago when the troubles between Greece and Turkey began. They say that these owners hang on to their property through sentiment or joint ownership, unable or unwilling to give them up. In far off climes they live fresh lives, but the old house roots them to the past and to their beginnings.

To get back to our 'find'. We were eating last Saturday night at The House of the Wind (aptly named in more ways than one). Thekla and her husband, Tassos, are the owners and both of them, together with their two sons, one son's fiancée, their daughter and son-in-law, were bustling to and fro all evening taking orders, serving food and generally putting their shoulders to the wheel the way Cypriot families do. It is the secret of their success, this family unity. Anyway, as the pace slackened a bit, we mentioned to Thekla that we were looking for a place to rent and were getting pretty fed up with what we have been shown. 'But I have a house!' she said, beaming at us over a pile of plates and empty cans of Keo beer. 'Come, I will take you.'

We followed her expensive-looking Land Rover down the hill in our small hired car and then, leaving both vehicles in the village car park, set off on foot down a narrow lane. An almost full moon lit our path. There was a deathly hush all about, it being about ten o'clock and the entire population fast in their beds. At the bottom of the lane where it turned at a right angle, high stone walls on either side of us, Thekla stopped and got out a key. The moonlight lit up some very ugly cement rendering on the exterior and an 'art deco' front door of awful yellow glass with chrome. Our spirits sagged. Why did Thekla's house happen to be the only one in the village, as far as we could see, with its pretty stonework covered in blobs of cement and with a chrome and glass front door?

Everything changed inside, however. We entered a small parlour and from that moved to a courtyard, high-walled, filled with moonlight and a giant bougainvillaea that tumbled from the balconies above. In a corner where the scarlet bougainvillaea could not reach it, stood a loquat tree.

'We'll take it,' we said.

'It grows above the sewer,' Thekla said, by way of explaining the success of her vine. 'Nice and quiet here?'

We agreed it was indeed very quiet.

We settled on the sum of one hundred and twenty pounds a month. It seemed very reasonable.

'You must not pay more than one hundred, Leez,' admonished our friend Anna, who runs the little hotel in the upper village.

'No, do not pay more than seventy,' says somebody else. They think we are very gullible and foolish. I will report later.

All love

Libby

6

P.S. You will notice my letter carries the extra, compulsory one cent stamp 'in aid of the refugees'. The refugees are never forgotten, except by careless foreigners and the thoughtless tourists who like to cross the UN buffer zone in Nicosia, pay for a day's visa, show their passports and peer about at what 'the wicked Turks are doing in the north'.

The refugees in question are, of course, the Greek Cypriots who were forced to flee their homes when Turkey invaded the north of the island in 1974. In the eyes of many Greek Cypriots Turkey seems to be blamed for the upheavals that changed forever the face of the island wherein the two Cypriot races had dwelt in relative harmony for hundreds of years. However, as clearly there is another side to the story, I have borrowed a book from a Nicosia library which deals with this whole sorry business and I hope to make myself au fait with these events as soon as our own domestic upheaval is over and life in a village gets under way. A donkey-trot pace of life should allow ample time for reading.

Nicosia

Tuesday

Thekla has assured us that she will clear her excess furniture out of the place before we move in. There is indeed rather a lot of it, mostly in what will be our dining room/sitting room. I have purchased a rubber 'plunger' from Woolworth's basement department, having been too carried away by the moonlight on Thekla's bougainvillaea to remember to check her plumbing. This, I reflect, could be rudimentary. I have also bought myself a giant-sized notepad to make a start on a proper diary, the standard ones looking too small for all the words I might be compelled to put down. To find such plebeian stores as Woolworth's on this romantic island of ours has been a bit of a shock, not to say a disappointment when here we are cheek by jowl with the mysterious Orient, so crusader-ridden, so rank with turbulent history! However, worries over drains are bound to occur.

Our Village

Saturday

Well, here we are!

I wish that this early entry could report a painless transition. Thekla's beds, adequate in their way, are not to blame. She has already apologized for the mattress on our bed having been left out, accidentally, in the rain. (So it does rain!) That was last March. No, the mattress is lumpy in parts, but those parts aren't strategic, really. What kept us up most of the night were other things. As we sat on the bed scratching our midge bites and listening to the dogs, we ruminated on Thekla's economy with the truth. A cacophony of yelps, yaps and howls assailed our ears from the valley below, only pausing to regroup and to snatch a little rest every hour or so.

'I'll talk to Nicos,' said Tim gloomily, as he switched on the light for the umpteenth time, swiping as he did so at a wayward mosquito with our expensive copy of *The Times* (Hilton bookshop). Midges are a different matter. They go underground, seeking out the softest parts of your anatomy, working their way through layers of cotton sheeting in the process, persistent, invisible and always triumphant.

'What use is Nicos?'

'He's the mukhtar's brother.'

We turned off the light, comforted by this thought. Nicos, taking pity on us as we staggered from the car park with our luggage yesterday, was a ray of hope.

Then the dogs, having been silent during the mosquito period, started up again...

Tuesday

A succession of bad nights. Anna has suggested we take vitamin B6 for the midges and beer, taken in generous quantities, she tells us, will settle the mosquitoes. She had no advice however, about the dogs and simply gave us one of her lugubrious shrugs as we poured out our woes, comforted by coffee taken with her at her hotel.

Anna, a new friend, has converted her hotel from the old market where once the village people brought their animals and farm produce. In the central courtyard she has built a small swimming pool, its turquoise blue set off by columns painted in a deep burnt sienna. Boxes of geraniums and trailing jasmine provide colour and scent, and potted plants make cool splashes of green. Inside the hotel Anna's good taste has made this little mountain retreat a place of simple comfort.

We have adopted Anna as a sort of Earth Mother, someone into whose kindly ear we can itemize our settling-in problems, and from whom we expect a helpful response. It is discouraging about the dogs, though. Anna's hotel, being fitted snugly into the centre of the upper village, is cocooned from such nuisances and Anna herself has far more pressing worries. We have got to know the life of her hotel intimately over the past months, having used it as our weekend retreat before we found our home. Today a party of twenty Scandinavians is arriving and the hotel water tank is dangerously low. The weather being extremely hot, they expect water in abundance. Can none of these Western Europeans ever be taught to understand that water in these parts is as precious as gold? No? Anna gives another shrug, her big brown eyes filled with resignation, her demeanour remains unflappable. She excuses herself and vanishes into her office, where two telephones are ringing simultaneously. There is no sign of her niece, the one who strums on a guitar in the foyer when she should be answering the phone. Neither is there any sign of the melancholy would-be actress, Panayiota, whose failure to appear in her capacity as

Assistant Manager is often noticeable. Panayiota is very beautiful, with a Marlene Dietrich languor about her. Next to water shortages, staffing problems come a close second in the daily hassles at the village hotel.

Sunday

Realizing that we can expect little practical help from Anna re the dogs, we are obliged to pin our hopes on our newly acquired 'lower village' friend, Nicos, who is the brother of our village mukhtar. 'Mukhtar' is the Turkish word for mayor (an anomaly accepted, apparently, by the Greek Cypriots, for many of whom all things Turkish are abhorrent).

It was a most pleasant surprise when Nicos turned up on our doorstep today, barely six days after our arrival, appearing like some genie from its bottle, intent on doing our bidding. He explained that as today is Sunday, he has been released from his handyman jobs around the village and can therefore give us his full attention. The three of us settled ourselves in the courtyard, the roof terrace being too hot at this time of day, with only the grapevine there to act as an umbrella. We told him that we cannot get a wink of sleep, the dogs are impossible.

'Christ, Liz! Don't y' know that there are hunters on this island? What d'ya expect them to hunt with, wolves?'

He laughs at his own joke, which sets off his smoker's cough. Nicos is ex-Liverpool, come home to his roots when years of toil in his fish and chip shop made him begin to realize that life should be for living. Besides, there were other things. He has hinted at these darkly but it is too soon in our acquaintance to go into details. Perhaps the hard work was secondary in importance to the sudden urgency to return to his roots.

'Well, yes,' we agree. 'We bought *The Cyprus Weekly* yesterday and noticed there's an article about these hunters. The Chairman of the Hunting Association was reported as saying that *forty-eight thousand* hunters on this small island is a national disaster. What do they shoot?'

'Anything that moves,' says Nicos carelessly. (Life in the United Kingdom has not, apparently, changed his Mediterranean attitudes towards wildlife.)

'I know they shoot partridges,' I tell him. 'Apparently the birds are so tame, being hand reared, that they're given no time to adapt to the wild. The hunters complain they may as well shoot at chickens! Then this article goes on to report that a rare vulture chick, carefully nursed into the wild by conservationists, has been shot. As there were only thirty left on the island, now there are twenty-nine!'

Nicos was sceptical. 'Who cares about bloomin' vultures?'

'To get back to the dogs.' Tim interrupts my flow before I get well and truly settled onto my soap box. 'Can your brother, the mukhtar, help us?'

'I'll have a word with him.'

Nicos' readiness to help with what is, very probably, a delicate matter, is gratifying.

'Of course, your house being 'ere, on the edge of the village, like, is bound to be noisier than anyone else's,' he assures us.

'That's not what Thekla told us,' I say crossly. 'Besides, what about our neighbours opposite? Not only must they be able to hear the woofing and the yapping and the howling down below, but they've got *two* dogs of their own next door to their bedroom, as far as we can tell. They could outdo Pavarotti, Carreras and Domingo without the slightest difficulty.'

Realizing that our friend has probably never heard of the trio, Tim asks, 'What makes them bark *all* night?'

'Maybe it's the snakes. Dogs don't like 'em.'

'Snakes?'

'Yes, surely you, Liz, a bloomin' Auzzie, must know about snakes?'

I agree I do. Tim looks alarmed.

'The snakes frighten the dogs. Some of the b— things are six

11

feet long or more. The black ones – they're OK. No need to worry about them, but mind the other fellers, the pale brown sort! Have you got boots?'

We haven't.

We cross the courtyard and lead our friend up the steps to our roof terrace.

'Well, you'll need 'em when you go down there.' Nicos waves vaguely at our stunning view. His Liverpudlian accent makes the whole scenario sound unreal, but worse, somehow. Boots hadn't entered into our scheme of things.

'Had a snake, poisonous sort, crawled up a ten-foot wall this summer,' he continues with relish. ''Ere in the village. Frightened Old Maria out of her wits, it did. She was up on the roof, hangin' out the washing.'

His gust of laughter sets off his smoker's cough once more. Tim pales. I realize that my London lounge lizard has a good deal to learn. After all, the poor dear is city bred – and English. Snakes have never entered into his lifestyle, unlike my mother, who takes them in her stride. Now well into her eighties, she dealt with one recently in the country garden of a friend. All that was needed was a spade and an unerring eye.

Tim, to calm his nerves, goes off to get himself and Nicos a beer. (Thekla's refrigerator, by some miracle, is working beautifully. If only the same thing could be said for the telephone, or come to that, the bathroom shower.)

Monday

Nicos was true to his word and this morning the mukhtar called. His many duties as mayor are interspersed with his work running the village coffee shop, a largely male preserve, open seven days a week. It was kind of him to come so promptly but as his English, unlike that of Nicos, is on a par with our Greek, we did not get very far. He is a portly, beaming fellow with thick spectacles.

We offered him Nescafé, not yet having mastered the art of the traditional coffee making. He declined, so we led him upstairs to the roof terrace. All three of us gazed out at the tranquil scene before us. On either side of us were the cascading hills and blue ridged mountains, in front a broad and peaceful valley opening out to a distant prospect of shimmering sea. Somewhere down there, tucked in amongst a group of almond trees, the ugly corrugated iron roofs of the dog sheds peeped out, some distance off but not far enough. Their occupants, worn out from their nightly concert, were resting. Not a drum was heard. Not a funeral note.

The mukhtar looked at us and shrugged. We shrugged back. With smiles and hearty handshakes all round, we descended to the ground floor and he left us.

'I intend to pursue this matter,' said Tim as the mukhtar's portly figure made its way up the lane. 'I am assured by Xenios that it is illegal to keep dogs in a village. Our friend the mukhtar knows that as well as anyone. If we can silence two of them, that will be a start.' But we already sense that we are on tricky ground; for sacred cow, substitute sacred dog.

To have an ally in Xenios, the holder of a high office in the legal world here, would be a bonus indeed. Already he and Tim, as fellow lawyers, have struck up a gratifying friendship. (Tim's assignment here is on a two and a half year basis. That seems a comfortable time in which to forget the future. To live for the day is enough.) Tim and I have managed to master the pronunciation of his name, to the great man's satisfaction. The letter 'x' is pronounced somewhere between a 'th' and a 'z', but to grapple with the spelling of his surname, which also starts with an 'x', takes practice. Xenios leads a life of frenetic activity more akin to living in London or Washington rather than on a remote island in the eastern Mediterranean.

Marooned far from home as we are on this far flung island, we feel more keenly the warmth of Xenios' obvious affection. Tim makes him laugh. So far I have seen little of the man, apart from

14

a quick coffee at the Hilton in Nicosia when he plied us with advice on all things Cypriot. Never, he advised, attempt to learn the language. Greek is the most difficult of all, and what is more, the village people speak the old classical Greek, more difficult still. This struck us as a little pessimistic. Xenios also advised us about doing business deals with his countrymen.

'You know what they say about the Greek, Tim my friend? No? Well they say that when you shake hands with one, check the number of fingers you have left.'

'Beware of Greeks bearing gifts?'

Xenios laughed. 'True, Eleezabeth, very true, or even this: I fear the Greeks even though they offer gifts.'

[This diary entry startles me as I read it now, looking back on what then seemed like Xenios, our new friend, having one of his jokes. However, we were to ignore this excellent piece of advice from Virgil via Xenios several years later, to our cost. One of our villagers, by dint of beguiling offers of home-made fruit cakes and jars of mulberry jam, managed to exchange the said gifts for some two thousand Cyprus pounds. But all that was in the future. We were convinced that all Cypriots were charming people, generous to a fault. In fact, to distrust them showed a fault in our own characters, and innocence was the order of the day.

Several weeks after our removal from Nicosia to the hills and in spite of bad nights with the dogs, we began to settle readily into village life. Here the skies were limitless and by night the stars were sharp and close. Close, too, were the hills. We felt all we needed to do was to lean from our roof terrace and brush them with our fingers. They ran away down and beyond, to grow into layer upon layer of folded mountains, the broad brown valley in the middle and the sea at the bottom, a long straight line of it, changing colour as the mountains changed. Our only current irritation (apart from the dogs, telephone and shower) was our

15

sitting room, or lack of it. This was a long, low-ceilinged room of charming proportions, entered from the courtyard, as was the kitchen and front 'parlour', its walls some eighteen inches thick with deep sills which, in time, would hold ornaments and dried flowers. The scarlet bougainvillaea peeped in through a courtyard window.

Wednesday

It is a fortnight today since Thekla promised to clear her possessions from our sitting room. So far we have been able to do little more than peer through its glass doors at the staggering array of goods within. Reminiscent of the tomb of Tutankhamun in the arrangement of its artefacts, but perhaps lacking the artistry and with no glitter of gold, it is a wondrous sight nonetheless. We can make out, stacked higgledy-piggledy, like the possessions of Pharaoh, a beach umbrella on its plastic stand, a car door (cream, saloon), a child's carry cot and pram and two giant-sized chandeliers with crimson silk shades. These appear to be balancing precariously on top of a wooden cabinet, one of whose glass doors is missing. Wooden cartons bulging with pieces of piping and flex, a spare wc bowl without a lid, a kitchen extractor fan and hood and a calor gas cylinder all fit snugly down one end of the room. At the other are ghostly shapes, armchairs etc., draped with what appear to be satin bedspreads decorated *à la chinoise*, with dragons. Other gifts left for the dead are several crates of wine which fill up the last vestiges of space.

Yes, yes. Do not worry. Everything will be cleared out 'after the wedding'.

To our surprise, no perhaps not to our surprise, we have been invited to this. It is next Saturday, the reception to be held at The House of the Wind.

'Come and watch us prepare the food,' said Thekla. 'I am preparing for two thousand people.'

16

Her hoarse voice, having delivered the invitations, hung up before I had time to register.

Two *thousand*?

Saturday

This morning, up at The House of the Wind, all is bustle. Tonight Thekla will be feeding the two thousand. Out on the terraces dozens of trestle tables and battalions of plastic chairs have been arranged for the banquet, the paper tablecloths anchored in place with metal clips, their tail ends fluttering in the breeze. The views from the terrace are even more spectacular than ours. One is tempted to throw a bread roll to see how far it would progress down the mountainside.

Behind the restaurant we find Thekla and her family hard at work. Several clay ovens, hired for the occasion, stand, igloo-like, on the backs of two lorries. Inside them their fires are already lit.

'Good, isn't it?' Thekla beams, her face flushed scarlet as she empties sackfuls of rice into the cauldrons of *tavas*. Her daughter, Stella, assisted by another woman, is emptying cans of tomatoes and trays of diced onions into the *stifado* to join the hefty hunks of lamb. Conscious of my own feelings of dither and inadequacy at the prospect of throwing a dinner party for eight, I marvel at these women's sang-froid.

Tassos, with a male assistant, is using long handled shovels to load trays of peeled potatoes into the fiery furnace. When each oven is filled, his assistant seals the doors with dollops of mud, which he slings with great nonchalance and accuracy at the cracks. Thekla explains, here the food will cook all day. Tassos pauses long enough to nod briefly in our direction and then to bellow ferociously at his small granddaughter, who is weaving dangerously between the adults' legs. As she passes by the spot where Tim and I are standing, she delivers a sharp and expert pinch on my right thigh. As this is the first occasion on which Thekla Junior and I

17

have become acquainted, I decide to make allowances. But there is a look in this three-year-old's eye that bodes ill. Were I her parents, I would pay attention.

That evening the wedding reception passed off without a hitch and all were fed thoroughly, to bursting point, in some cases. From long practice Thekla had got her quantities right. Not one to stand on ceremony, the Cypriot attacks his food without preliminaries and with gusto. As much food as that on the plates may end up on the tablecloth. The bridal couple, busy receiving guests, appeared to miss out on the banquet entirely. They stood with commendable patience for nearly three hours as the interminable line of guests queued patiently to pay its respects. When all were seated and fed and it was time for bride and groom to take the floor, a trio of musicians, lodged under a giant grapevine, struck up. Bit by bit the bridal gown began to disappear beneath a welter of bank notes, as well-wishers stepped forward to pin their gifts on to the shimmering bridal satin. In this way a pair may start their married life with a hefty slice taken out of the mortgage. Others joined the dance, the men breaking off to dance with each other, the women doing likewise, arms uplifted, each keeping time to the music's hypnotic beat. Slowly the pace began to quicken, hearts and steps beat faster and soon all were circling and stamping to the change of pace and mood. The stars spun in an inky sky, the three musicians lost themselves in an orgy of sound, the small children gazed in wonder, babies slept in prams or on fathers' shoulders, and the young bride and groom, as beautiful as film stars, danced on. Tim and I, too shy to join in, stood on the sidelines until sleepiness overcame us and we wended our way down the chalky hillside to our new home, the village already taking on a welcoming appearance as we walked down our lane and let ourselves in through our yellow glass door. Below in the valley the dogs were silent, lulled into drowsiness by the music beating softly down from The House of the Wind.

SEPTEMBER

Monday

A tiring day! At four o'clock Tassos appeared. He had brought his utility truck as far down our lane as he could go without getting himself wedged fast between its high stone walls. With him were his second son, Christakis, and Christakis' young fiancée. They look far too young to be leaving school, let alone getting married. But that is how it is done here, we are told. A young man takes an interest in a girl and the moment they start 'walking out' they are as good as married. In fact it is not uncommon, when the wedding bells ring out, for a bride to be in the family way.

All three set to work with a will. As Cypriot women are expected to do the work of donkeys, Christakis' young bride-to-be shouldered an armchair single-handed, frail as she was. I hoped she wasn't in a certain condition. She was followed by her fiancé and her future father-in-law manoeuvring the wooden cabinet.

After a while, our phone rang. It was Thekla. I had forgotten all about Melanie, the new cleaning woman that Thekla had recommended. Could someone please pick her up? Melanie had finished her other job higher up the mountain and was 'ready'. I explained that Tim had our car and was still out. Could Christakis go then? Thekla asked. I explained that he had just left with the first load of her furniture. Thekla hung up. At six fifteen or so Chris returned but was adamant that he could not fetch Melanie. Why couldn't his mother do it? I explained that his mother could not leave the restaurant, a fact of which he was well aware. September is one of their busiest months. Chris vanished out of the door beneath a giant-sized sofa on which his fiancée had straddled the baby's pram. The phone went again. Thekla reported that Melanie had left her last address and was making her way, on foot, to The House of the Wind. 'She was comin' round the mountain', in fact.

'I'll ask Tim to fetch her as soon as he gets back,' I told her. 'He shouldn't be long.'

'*Efkaristo*,' said Thekla and hung up.

As the last items of furniture disappeared into the truck, I buttonholed Tassos. Reluctantly he followed me into our bathroom, which is located beside the front door. Here we were joined by a large, middle-aged man, who is, presumably, a neighbour, though we have not, as yet, been introduced.

All three of us watched while I demonstrated what happens when our shower is turned on. We stood, shoulder to shoulder, in the small mini-lake which this action produced.

Tassos feigned incomprehension, anxious to get home. Fortunately the neighbour was ready to understand the problem. He translated in rapid Greek. I thanked him with many *efkaristos*.

'*Endaxi*,' said Tassos cheerfully and dashed out, springing into his truck, in the back of which the glass cabinet stood tall and proud. He got ready to back at speed up the lane. From my vantage point by the front door I could see what he could not. (The helpful neighbour had now disappeared.) There was a tearing sound and before I could shriek 'stop!' several pieces of plaster fell from both our opposite neighbour's front wall and ours, taking a tangle of electric cable with it. This had wrapped itself around the top of the offending cabinet and bits of it had fallen in loops over the truck's bonnet.

I dashed indoors to check that our phone was not one of the casualties. Surprisingly, the phone gave its familiar buzz. Then it rang. I reassured Thekla that I had just spotted Tim coming down the lane. He would fetch Melanie.

Upstairs on our roof terrace, Tassos dealt with the outcome of his careless haste. Grabbing the cat's cradle of electric wiring, he applied a rapid tourniquet and, hooking it on to a piece of the grape trellis, he bounded downstairs, apparently satisfied that he had re-connected us to the outside world again. With the surplus wires now clear of the cabinet, but only just, Tassos leapt back into his truck. Opposite us, our neighbour watched impassively

from her doorstep. I closed my eyes as the engine revved violently, the truck reversed and our precious new pots of geraniums looked doomed to extinction. Many geraniums, in kerosene tins painted in pretty colours, edge our lane as far up as the car park. This time they survived.

I went indoors and poured myself a stiff Cyprus vodka. Excellent stuff and very cheap. Then the doorbell rang. It was Melanie. She stood in the doorway beaming, her portly figure and face still perspiring gently from her walk. Tim's lean figure in his five dollar yellow trousers loomed behind her.

'I am come to help you. We will be friends,' she announced.

I hope we will, although anyone who is able to replace the incomparable Mrs C. I left behind would be a real find. 'Cling to a good husband – or a good cleaning woman – with hoops of steel,' my mother used to tell us.

'Where you want that I begin?' Melanie asked, plonking her enormous dilly bag on a shelf in the front parlour, all but dislodging my treasured photograph of myself with the Pope. I straightened the photograph and suggested she put her bag on a chair.

'But your head. You have a black scarf over yourself, but you are smiling! Are you a widow?' Melanie leant heavily towards the photo, peering closely.

'No,' I replied stiffly, catching Tim's grin from the kitchen door.

Melanie took the hint. 'Now I am going to make your house nice and clean. Where I start, up or down?'

We entered the sitting room, so recently cleared of Thekla's belongings.

'This room is very dirty. Maybe I do it next week.'

Much as cleaning women unnerve me, I stuck to my guns.

'No. Now. Today, please,' I told her firmly.

'I must therefore have water,' said Melanie, removing her shoes.

I said there was a tap outside in the lane but I wasn't sure whether or not we were allowed to use it.

Melanie paddled in bare feet to the front door and an excited shouting match followed. She returned, looking sober. The neighbours need the water for the sheep. The English couple can use their own!

'They are very bad people,' observed Melanie.

We found a useable tap behind the loquat tree.

Tim passed a precious bucket of water across the courtyard to Melanie, who hurled it into the sitting room and demanded more. Soon the ugly tiled floor was awash while we looked on nervously. Would the mukhtar come and arrest us? Melanie was quite unconcerned, however. She drenched the shelves, doors and windows with more and more buckets and then, satisfied with her efforts in this area, grabbed a broom. With surprising agility for someone so rotund she charged at the ceiling, taking beetles, moths, spiders and cobwebs and whatever else in her wake. Tearing up one of Thekla's old tablecloths that had served as a dust sheet, she lunged at the windows and began a violent polishing attack on their grimy panes. She was in there for two hours, the agreed length of her stay. Meanwhile Tim and I retired to the kitchen. After a while, Melanie joined us at our supper, perching herself on the edge of the table and helping herself to a tomato and several raw carrots. As she ate, replenishing herself from time to time, she chatted. Then, removing an apple, she returned to her work.

'Do you think we really need her?' Tim asked.

'I'm not sure.'

'She uses an awful lot of water,' he said thoughtfully.

'Yes, and quite a lot of carrots. I was keeping those large ones for old Demetri's donkey.'

Sunday

My writing has gone by the board these past days, what with the heat and the dogs. Any thought of having a sleep in on Sundays is soon vanquished by the bells which sound off at 6 a.m. and then repeat themselves at 7 a.m. in case you'd dozed off again.

By 7.15 or so the first sprinkling of worshippers is hurrying by, the women's shoes making a *clip-clopping* on the stones as they pass our house. I decided to join them and asked Tim if he would come. Several cups of strong coffee had not helped his splitting head.

'You won't understand a word,' he muttered as he put several slices of bread into the toaster.

'Nevertheless, I'm going,' I told him. 'May be if I pray hard enough a miracle might happen.'

I entered the side door of the lovely stone church that perches on the lip of the valley at the end of our lane. Conscious of all eyes upon me and feeling a little embarrassed, I popped a twenty cent coin into the offertory plate and selected two candles. One candle was for us. The other was for the dogs. The heftiest candles cost one pound but I reckoned that the Almighty was not too fussy. There was a sand tray nearby, held aloft in an ornate gilded sconce, and in this, after lighting my candles from another, I placed my modest offerings. All the ladies were at the back while a handful of men, mostly elderly, sat at the front. I caught Myafora's eye and she beckoned me to sit by her. (Myafora is our next-door neighbour Evagora's mother and lives next door to her.)

It was true what Tim had said, of course, but the hypnotic chanting of the priest and his assistant had a calming effect on my jangling nerves. Occasionally, as the service moved into its second hour and then another half, a murmur of chattering fluttered along our rows of high-backed seats, with the occasional diversion of a new arrival – a mother with her child in a pushchair, an elderly lady with two sticks. Once or twice the priest, breaking off from his devotions, cast a threatening eye in our direction and silenced the miscreants with a hiss. On one occasion, this gesture was backed up by his wife, a formidable woman in a dark headscarf and flat-heeled pumps that *scuff-scuffed* on the tiled floor as she went about her duties. These included producing a breadknife from a drawer beneath the offertory table and slicing up several giant circular loaves, which were then stacked on another table by

25

the altar steps. I watched, fascinated, as, clasping each loaf to her bony chest, she proceeded to cut it. My thoughts wandered to the story my mother used to tell us of the Queensland housewife dying from a stab wound received in dealing with a recalcitrant pumpkin, held in like manner.

As the candles flickered and the soft lamps glowed, I prayed to the Almighty that our dumb friends down in the valley might be silenced and become truly dumb again. As an addendum, I suggested to the Almighty that He might persuade the owners to feed the poor things and thus make us all happy.

Tim and I were up for a good deal of last night and indeed into the early hours of this morning. At about 4 a.m. Tim had said 'I'm going out!'

Forbearing to switch on the light in a fruitless act of consideration, he grabbed the first garment that came to hand and vanished downstairs. I followed, but instead went out on to the roof terrace that leads off our bedroom. Tim's tall form was already making its way up the lane, the rays from the one street light giving my Chinese dressing gown 'a more than oriental splendour'. Tim's thin legs stuck out for a good metre below the hem, ending in a pair of white cotton Hilton scuffs. The flimsiness of the scuffs hindered his military style somewhat, but he soldiered bravely on, his brown Fedora tipped menacingly forwards. My view was now hindered by high walls but Tim's cultured tones came forth clearly enough.

'If you don't b— well get your dogs to b— well stop this racket, I'll do so myself!'

A torrent of guttural Greek, like shots from a Kalashnikov, greeted this remark. Then three or four figures in jungle greens edged into the lamplight. What on earth were they doing at four o'clock in the morning? Two women in shortie nighties now appeared in the doorway opposite and our neighbour, Evagora, left her mattress on the roof and began busying herself in her kitchen downstairs. Half the village appeared to be up. A man in pyjama trousers with bare chest joined the shortie nighties.

Tim had been practising the next phrase for some days. '*Thelo issihia!*'

A fresh burst of Kalashnikov followed. This stab at the local lingo did not seem to impress. One of the jungle greens waved a double barrelled shotgun in a menacing fashion.

'You'd look more intimidating in trousers,' I hissed over the balcony. 'Besides, I don't think they understand your Greek.'

I was wrong, on both counts.

'You can sleep in the daytime,' shouted the largest of the jungle greens, a beefy fellow with legs like tree trunks. 'Plenty of time. You sleep then!'

This was too much. I had a sudden inspiration.

'He is an advocate!' I shrieked.

The effect was startling. In a flash front doors closed, lights went out and the green brigade disappeared up the lane. Even the dogs were impressed. A deathly hush descended over all.

'Do you think it was the dressing gown that did it?' I managed to giggle as, at 4.30 a.m., we climbed back into bed.

Friday

Apart from the incident in the dressing gown the other night, Tim has shown commendable self-control during our initiation into village life. After all, he must get off to work well before eight o'clock. Tim works as an Advisor to an International Law Conference to be held here in the millennium year. This takes him north to Nicosia and south to Limassol, both some forty minutes away by car. We have bought a second-hand Japanese car, a little Mazda, which is cream coloured and economical with petrol. What could be a more delightful way of commuting to one's work than coasting down the mountain, barely changing gear before one reaches the bottom, swooping round bends, each one of which provides broad and differing vistas of un-polluted landscape? Once the highway is reached, there is a certain amount of traffic to be sure, but this is a minor irritation until the outskirts of town are reached. All along these highways bloom, for month after drought-stricken month, the hardy oleander, set in cement troughs down the middle, nodding its pink and white blooms in defiance of all lack of H_2O. How do they survive so successfully?

Today Tim has gone off in his pin-striped, seersucker suit and imitation panama hat, bought at a Sydney market before we left Australia in July. The latter cost one Australian dollar and is earning its keep in all this heat. Watching his lanky form plod up the lane, I noticed a fresh rash of bougainvillaea blossom all over 'our' part of the lane. I set to with a broom, well aware that, Evagora and the other ladies have done their outdoor chores hours ago. The blossoms being too beautiful to throw into the dustbin, I placed some into one of Thekla's cut glass bowls where they make a welcome splash of colour in our newly cleaned and sparkling sitting room.

Until our furniture arrives from Sydney in a couple of months, we are reliant for decoration on one or two icons of the usual dour type, and that is about it. Our things are to come by sea, a protracted business. Meantime, we are making do with a heavy chocolate brown table (removed from the kitchen to be used as a dining table) and four upright village chairs with woven cane seats (picturesque but unsympathetic to the posterior). There are three armchairs upholstered in a hectic orange. The grey-tiled sitting room floor positively sparkles since Melanie's efforts, as do the window frames and glass door that leads into the courtyard. As the kitchen and parlour doors are also made of glass, the ground floor rooms are light and cheerful. This is not always true of Cypriot houses, whose high-walled courtyards, built for coolness, tend to darken the adjoining rooms. This simple cottage, with its cool, white-painted courtyard and steps that lead to the floor above, its homeliness, its airy views, suits my longing to escape from our consumer-driven world. The dozen or so village cars are kept in the car park at the top of the village so that our little lanes are free of parked vehicles or ugly meters. Slow and easy. That's it.

Saturday

Relations with our neighbours being somewhat strained at the moment, I ventured into the lane with my broom a good deal earlier than usual. Evagora was at her daily ritual but our neighbour over the way was busying herself indoors, judging by the clatter coming from her courtyard. It seemed prudent to try a little cementing of relationships, particularly since we have discovered that some hunting dogs belong to Evagora's husband, Andrea, and several to his sons.

I congratulated Evagora (sincerely) on her tubs of geraniums, which march in a row and join her mother's lot next door.

'You should cut that back,' she replied, ignoring the compliment. 'Tim could do it. I can lend him a saw.' Evagora's English is good, some years of her childhood having been spent in England.

I decided to ignore Evagora's advice, as Thekla's pride and joy has now become ours and ten minutes' housework on the blossoms seems a small price to pay for the vision of glory that greets the eye as we wake up each morning. Tendrils of bloom creep horizontally along the verandah railings outside our bedroom and fountains and cascades of scarlet tumble overboard into the lane and downwards into the courtyard below. Where the sun greets them the colours change to varying shades of pink.

'You speak such good English, Evagora.' The compliment was well meant as well as an attempt at changing the subject. 'How long did you live in England?'

'Long enough,' replied my neighbour with a laugh. 'So cold! I'll never forget that awful cold. My sister's still there. I feel really sorry for her, poor thing.'

The sun was now getting too hot for outdoor chores and I went indoors, after accepting Evagora's offer of some Cyprus coffee.

29

This is made thus: a teaspoon or two of coffee grounds are placed in a tiny long-handled metal pot, to which water is added. This is then brought to the boil over a flame and quickly removed. The coffee is served according to taste and is surprisingly refreshing on a hot day.

Perhaps the dog problem will resolve itself, I mused as I went upstairs to tidy up. A small group of women, including Evagora, assemble each morning early to pop their children on to the school bus. Later in the day they cluster under the mulberry tree by the car park for the arrival of the bread van. The round loaves of bread are the size of frisbees but a good deal heftier and, should one have the strength and accuracy to hurl a loaf, concussion could well result were the target human. Stale loaves are fed to the dogs, poor things. Bread seems to make up a large part of their diet. No wonder they complain so loudly.

Monday

I have discovered already that a large part of the villagers' daily needs are met by 'the men in vans'. One day the butcher calls, another the man who sells fresh chickens (though the word 'chicken' is a slight misnomer). Two greengrocer's vans vie with each other daily, while the dry cleaner comes on Fridays and the man with clothes to sell appears now and then. As times for these appearances are fluid, a loud honking of horns heralds the arrival of a trader. However, I am too far away to hear this and have missed several useful visits to the greengrocer's van. The women who live by the car park have an advantage, but sooner or later the rest appear, the older women in their perennial black stockings and (for church) headscarves to match, while the pitiless sun beats down on their unsuitable attire. Once in mourning, always in mourning, seems to be the way the women view their obligations. The men get by with a black armband which is later discarded.

Tim's peace offering after the dog fracas has been to present a

small plastic rocking horse to the village playground. He found it in a second-hand shop. It will be interesting to see how long it survives.

The playground, beside the car park, occupies land until recently the property of the Greek Orthodox Church and rumour has it that the villagers had quite a difficult and protracted tussle with the authorities in gaining this concession. The piece of land thus wrenched is a small space, beyond which is the tiny Byzantine chapel of Ayios Michaelis, the oldest of our village's five chapels. Built with the lovely local stone, now browned with age, its stony-faced frescoes, tenth century or thereabouts, gaze sternly from the walls in the dim, religious light. Although the visitor is free to enter at any time, the chapel is rarely used, except to mark the birthday of its original namesake and that of those Cypriots who bear his name.

Nearer to the children's playground, on a more pedestrian level, are two public wcs, put there for the use of tourists, not nearly enough of whom visit our small village but concentrate on the great variety of shops up the hill. While coachloads of foreigners – French, German, British, Belgian, Russians (in increasing numbers) and others grind their way up the mountain each day of summer, in full view of the rest of us, we are fortunate to cream off one coachload or the occasional rented car load. Evagora is convinced that the coach drivers are in cahoots with the shopkeepers aloft, and Chrisso, the mukhtar's wife, Koulla and others agree. These ladies devote each afternoon to their stitching, perched on low chairs outside the one or two shops or outside their houses, producing linen 'lace' of exquisite artistry. With the arrival of a likely customer, a healthy rivalry exists to entice him or her into the net.

Tuesday

It is not long before friends and relations, aware that we have settled in a place that promises to be different and/or interesting, begin to sit up and take notice.

A telephone call today from Roslyn in Gloucestershire.

'Libby *darling*! How *exciting* you're in Cyprus! May I come out?'

Knowing it was just a matter of time before I heard from this cousin of mine, but nevertheless hoping for a little more leeway with the unpacking, I said, 'Yes – um – when?'

'Next month. I so *badly* need a holiday! Will the weather still be warm about the twentieth? I *must* have a break.'

'Is something the matter?' I asked, wondering why Roslyn, of all people, should be in need of a holiday when her life seems nothing but.

'My eczema, it has spread up my legs and is now all over my arms!'

'How awful for you! How did you get it?'

'It's Cook. Did you meet Mavis when you were here at Easter? No, perhaps you didn't. She is driving me to *distraction*. A daily dip in the sea is just what I need.'

'Well, we're not by the sea. We're in the mountains,' I began but Roslyn was already well advanced with her plans: We can all have a week by the seaside. We'll take an apartment. Such fun! As for the week she'll spend in the mountains, her visit will be more successful if she can stay at a nearby hotel. (Has someone told her about the dogs – and the plumbing?)

'All right Roslyn, old thing,' I managed. 'I'll look for an apartment for one week and will book you into our village hotel for the other. Is that all right?'

'Perfect,' she said happily and hung up before the old familiar exasperation with my cousin began rising in my breast. An apartment by the sea is most definitely not what either Tim or I have contemplated, not for some considerable time at least, and the whole thing will be an entirely unwarranted expense.

Friday

An unfamiliar voice on the telephone this morning.

'Mr Timotheos?' it said.

'No. He is not here. May I take a message?'

'It is about the donkey. We go to see the donkey on Sunday.'

'What donkey?'

'Mr Timotheos, he buy a donkey.' The male voice at the other end of the phone hesitated. 'The donkey his name is Calif,' he explained. 'She is a man donkey.'

Speechless for a moment or two, I waited for further enlightenment, but it did not come. The caller assured me once again that the donkey's name was indeed Calif. Did I not like man donkeys? Perhaps we would prefer a female?

'Hullo? Hullo?' said the voice.

This evening, on his return, Tim looked coy.

'Yes, well, you always said you'd like a donkey.'

'Honestly, what has possessed you? You'll have to tell this fellow the deal is off. Besides, where would we put it?'

'Old Demetri might keep it for you.'

'You mean us,' I corrected.

'Yes. Well, you tell me you've already made friends with his wife – Crystalla, isn't it? Let's go and talk to them tomorrow. Isn't his donkey the one that ate our chrysanthemums?'

'If you're trying to talk me round to keeping donkeys, you're not going the right way about it. That tub of chrysanthemums was, as you very well know, my pride and joy.'

I climbed into bed early and this is where I am finishing today's entry. Tim is reading downstairs, in our newly cleansed sitting room, and trying to look nonchalant. The midges after sundown drive us off the roof terrace, which is sad, these starry evenings being so filled with magic. I am distinctly annoyed. How can we straddle the double hurdles of asking a favour of an elderly couple we have barely got to know (smiling and nodding terms only) to explain our peculiar (and possibly impertinent) request, in Greek? In my annoyance I have forgotten to ask Tim if he has irrevocably clinched the deal.

My friendship with our elderly neighbours, Crystalla and Demetri, grows rapidly as time goes by, and my pathetic attempts at Greek bring much merriment. Crystalla is on her own on weekdays and with her bad heart is only able to do a few basic chores. Demetri, in his eighty-sixth year, is in fine fettle, hand-ploughing his few acres with his donkey's help, tending his vegetable plot, his orchard and his chickens. Once these matters are seen to he is to be found with his friends at the coffee house. Crystalla, meanwhile, takes up her position at her favourite spot under the grapevine. Here she and I while away the hot afternoons to the accompanying sounds of scratching hens and the cooing of her five white doves. Her small house and paved, unwalled garden, being on the edge of the village, have views as fine as ours.

Conversation being limited, we enjoy each other's silences. The old lady wears spectacles with extremely thick lenses, her poor eyesight very probably due to years of stitching the fine 'lace' work. In her black stockings and black dress, she sits with gnarled hands folded on her apron, rocking with mirth at my attempt to learn new words. My inability to pronounce the Greek word for 'rooster' (or was it 'chickens'?) never ceases to make her chuckle. Her generosity is touching and we tuck into her wonderful figs and the produce from Demetri's garden, such as sweet corn cobs. When the oranges and mandarins and lemons grow ripe I am instructed to help myself, at any time. The children of the old couple, apart from the son who has emigrated to the States, turn up on weekends, Sunday, in particular, being a family day.

Saturday

A successful day. We found Old Demetri in his orchard by the fowl run. He was picking figs with one of his sons, who introduced himself as Agamemnon. The latter is a charming fellow and explained that he perfected his English while working for the Cyprus Tourist Board in London. This is a huge relief. After a few polite preliminaries, I nudged Tim in the ribs and encouraged by the friendly smiles, he explained our problem. We (he) had gone and agreed to buy a donkey tomorrow and what did Agamemnon and Demetri think about it? Could we keep our donkey with Demetri's donkey, and naturally all costs would be met by us? We didn't want to be a nuisance, of course.

As Agamemnon explained all this to his father a slow grin spread across the old man's weather-beaten face, a look of huge amusement. Well, thank goodness, he was taking it in good part. A further short dialogue in Greek followed and then, with great solemnity, fitting to the occasion, Agamemnon spoke.

'My father, he says you may share his donkey. Come, we will go and see.' Agamemnon's voice has a soft, sing song quality and we followed eagerly. There was something comforting in the idea that a donkey shared was a trouble halved.

We followed the two men down the hill, Demetri as spritely as his son. We skirted a stone wall and found the donkey in question in a small yard, an old door serving as a gate. A home-made shed with a corrugated iron roof provided shelter in bad weather.

'My father, he says it is better you use this donkey,' Agamemnon said gently but firmly, as though mad dogs and Englishmen were daily occurrences in his life.

'See, she is very nice. She is a good donkey. She is born here. Her name is Madonna.'

Madonna has eyes and nose as soft as moss. Her demeanour, chrysanthemums notwithstanding, is all innocence. To demonstrate his point, Agamemnon leapt on her back, stroked her ears and gently pulled her tail. Old Demetri grinned happily.

'My father says you may have his donkey whenever you like. It is better. The other donkey, he might not be kind to you. He might kick.'

Tim looked alarmed. Only once has he ever been near anything on four hooves and on that occasion the animal bolted with him into the Egyptian desert. Misconstruing my silence, if not Tim's, Agamemnon continued.

'She is tidier and cleaner than any dog,' he told us earnestly. 'She will take us wherever we like to go. She will take us up to the big village or down the valley, and when we are tired, do not worry, she will bring us home again.'

We are honoured and touched by such generosity. We assure Agamemnon that we will help pay for her food etc. Agamemnon will not hear of this. No, Madonna will eat the hay from the field.

'What about a saddle?' I asked, half jokingly.

'We will try to find you a good saddle, of course. There are not many people in Cyprus making such things now. Before, there were many donkeys in the villages. They were living in the houses. Now the government will not allow this.'

Old Demetri dug out from under a stack of parsley hay a home-made saddle and halter together with an ancient saddlebag.

'We will get you a better one,' said his son. 'It is necessary that Madonna is dressed nicely for you.'

The saddle, made of sacking and lengths of wood, certainly looks guaranteed to slip the most unsuspecting disc.

'Riding a donkey is not the same as riding a horse,' said Anna when I recounted the day's doings over the phone. 'It is very bump when you go down the hill.'

Monday

A number of people here having told us that there is one other expatriate (English) couple in our village, I decided to pay a call. We have been here for nearly a month. Although the village is small, neither Tim nor I have caught sight of them. A little English conversation is what I thirst for when Tim is away all day. My *kalimeras* and *kalisperas* are beginning to wear a bit thin.

Chrisso, the mukhtar's wife, directed me up the lane and then along another narrow lane past a tiny stone chapel. The English couple's house overhangs this lane, a sheer wall rising up to two storeys, but windowless. The view upstairs would be glorious but the government's strict building regulations must have something to do with it. Any house that is being restored must copy exactly the original dwelling.

There was no bell on the tall wooden gates that led into the courtyard so I lifted the latch and entered.

'Is this a good moment to call?' I enquired in what I hoped was not too hearty a tone (after all, they are English).

'No, it isn't!'

The voice seemed to be coming from the kitchen, where a clattering of pans followed. Regretting my neighbourly act, I retreated towards the gate, but then the husband of the Kitchen Voice appeared. Clearly embarrassed, he ushered me towards a room which led off the courtyard. It had once been the all-purpose family room of the traditional old house, spacious and high-ceilinged. Now, restoration had done its work and, in place of the old hand-cut beams and a ceiling made from interwoven twigs, was a glossy new effect with machine-cut rafters, plaster and paint. The exterior stonework of the house had lost its 'hand-made' charm through too much pointing, giving the whole an appearance of rigorous modernity.

The husband and I made polite conversation, which was interrupted at one point by the appearance of his wife, who left some iced drink on the coffee table beside me and then vanished back to her kitchen. I had selected an upright chair which, under the circumstances, seemed more prudent than the choice of one of their vast, inescapable armchairs. The husband explained that they were expecting their Greek tutor for supper

and that he was due any minute. They have been living here for several years and find the language taxing, but are persevering nonetheless. Perhaps the prospect of the forthcoming struggle in not only dealing with the language, but also with its instructor, was the reason for the wife's ill temper. However, finishing my drink as rapidly as possible, I bade my farewells to the husband and left.

Monday

It has been clear for some weeks that we need two cars, my Mazda having to make do for both of us at the moment. Tim spotted an old Rover (1960s) at a dealer's in Nicosia the other day and found it irresistible. Heavy on petrol, it grinds up the mountain like a tank, using up more than its fair share of the world's resources. However, his pride in it is inordinate.

OCTOBER

Wednesday

Today, 1st October, is Cyprus Independence Day. Independence was granted to the island by Britain on 16th August 1960 on condition that Britain kept two sovereign bases here.

Thursday

I have made a number of friends in the upper village. This is cheering. As they are too busy with their lace making and selling to come to me, I go to them. It being too hot to walk, I drive up to the upper village, though the distance is barely a mile, but steep. There is always an extra chair on the pavement, a cup of coffee or a drink of orange juice to welcome me. There is also the shared interest of spotting and trapping the wandering tourist, most of whom wear anxious expressions as they are hustled by indecision, aggravated by a shortage of time. Their coach driver has a heavy schedule of sightseeing planned for them. These are the package tourists. The more independent, arriving in their rented cars, can afford to wander at leisure, the astute among them able to spot the good stuff, the real linen, from the Chinese cotton imports.

'They will not buy,' says Marina as we sit side by side on the pavement on our miniature chairs, the sun beating down like a ton weight, the weary tourists drifting past. Behind us rows of tablecloths, mats and runners hang like washing.

'How do you know?' I ask, curious.

'They are French.' Marina's voice is contemptuous.

'I could have sworn they were British. Just look at those knees!'

The object of scrutiny are two women in crimplene dresses, plastic sandals and straw hats who, having passed our shop, settle

41

themselves on the verandah of the café opposite, revealing as they do so four remarkably pallid joints below the crimplene.

A Russian couple pass, the girl unusually dark and very beautiful. Andreas, Marina's husband, pounces with all the expertise of long practice. Five minutes later the couple emerge from his shop and are on their way again.

'These Russians are very strange people. I do not understand them.'

Andreas' benevolent face is creased up now. In spite of years in the rough and tumble of commerce he is offended.

'What is the matter with these people? I will tell you! Communism! That's what the matter is. They have no manners because they are brought up under Communism. One minute they talk to you and while you talk they walk out! Russians, they have money. Plenty money. But no manners. They are still Communists!'

Marina, philosophical, takes up her embroidery again. I never tire of watching these women at their work. The intricate 'lace-making' is achieved by cutting tiny squares in the Irish linen, counting each thread with the point of even tinier scissors. The designs are never stencilled on, the women relying solely on their expertise. Never have I seen one false thread drawn, one square cut off-centre. It is an art brought, it is thought, by the Venetians, who occupied the island in the late fifteenth to the sixteenth centuries. Escaping the heat of Nicosia, the ladies brought this work with them when they built their summer residences in the hills. Leonardo da Vinci, who visited Cyprus in 1481, has given his name to one of the most popular of these designs. It is said he took a piece of lace as a gift for the high altar of Milan Cathedral.

Silverware is also made by the village people, the men making items for the church and the household and the women making the fine filigree. These artisans are not above doing repair work for a customer, and the sounds of gentle hammering and tapping will lead you down some narrow alleyway to their workshops. These often appear cramped and dark but today I collected my silver hairbrush from one of them and am delighted with the neat work that has been done.

Monday

'Droulla, I have brought you some grapes.'
'Oh not this morning, Liz. It is too hot. This afternoon maybe.'
I have three bags in the car full of grapes. They weigh a ton. This October weather, which seems as hot as August, is speeding the ripening process to such an extent that I must get rid of the grapes before the wasps do. Our vine overhanging the roof terrace is heavy with bunches so thick I am getting desperate.

I lug my grapes into the Popular Bank. George, who hates Mondays, gives me a bleary smile, stamps my passbook and hands it back.

'What about my money, George?'
'Oh yes, yes. Sorry, sorry!'
Thinking to brighten his day, I ask him about the grapes.
'I am eating the grapes every day. My wife, she is eating them. My children also. We are eating grapes all the time.'
I walk to the hotel. Anna is at her morning deskwork, as usual.
'Anna, would you like these for your guests?'
'No, Leez.'
'But we've got so many! Thekla doesn't seem to want them either. We can't just waste them!'
'Everybody has grapes. Cyprus has too many grapes,' says Anna heavily. She gives one of her philosophical shrugs that have mitigated at least half a dozen crises at the hotel since our first acquaintance.

I continue on to the post office.
'Michaelis, would you like some grapes?'
Michaelis replies in his soft, rapid Greek. It is clear that he has many grapes of his own. However, he comes up with the first helpful suggestion so far. I should go and see the Mayor.

43

The Municipal Building is one of the handsomest in the upper village. Built in the best British Colonial style, it occupies a central position. There is an imposing stone gateway. I pass through it and a young man emerges from an office and we exchange *kalimeras*. He has a bundle of papers under one arm, is clearly in a rush but graciously ushers me into his office. His assistant follows. I explain about the grapes, feeling a little foolish. Would the old people at the Home like them? The young man thinks they would. How much would I be asking? I explain hurriedly that I want no payment. They are a gift. Both municipal employees look surprised.

The assistant, whose name is Anastasia, writes down my name and telephone number. 'And what is your name?' I ask the handsome young man.

'My name is Sophocles. I am the Mayor. You have heard of Sophocles?'

I hide my surprise. 'Of course.'

(Can anyone so young and handsome really be a mayor? For some reason he is not using the title of mukhtar. I suspect he rather fancies himself as westernized.)

'Everyone has heard of Sophocles,' I tell him. 'You are famous.'

We both enjoy the little joke. Mr Sophocles presses a card into my hand and assures me that everything will be arranged. A municipal truck will come to collect my grapes. In the meantime, should we wish an interview it would be best to arrange an appointment. He is very busy and about to leave for Athens. He begins stuffing his papers into a giant briefcase. I take the hint and leave.

I am thankful that there is someone in one of our villages who believes in making appointments. Perhaps I will call again.

Tuesday

Our summer is on the wane and the whole country is gasping under a thin white dust, longing for the first good thunderstorm.

Since the episode last month with Tassos and his removals truck, we have kept a wary eye on the cat's cradle of wires hanging from the grape trellis. (I gather that the name Tassos should be pronounced as Dassos.)

Yesterday Mr Stephanopolous, the only electrician in either village, turned up to install a second telephone upstairs. This has meant a six-week wait. As we needed to explain to Mr Stephanopolous that we would like our new answerphone installed at the same time, Thekla's daughter, Stella, agreed to step in as interpreter. This done, I left him to it. Halfway through proceedings, I took him his morning cup of coffee and we both beamed with satisfaction at the new phone installed on my bedside table. I went next door on some errand, leaving Mr Stephanopolous to install the answerphone downstairs, confident that he had grasped Stella's instructions. On re-entering the house, I found Mr Stephanopolous had gone and the answerphone was *not* downstairs but upstairs on the bedroom floor, attached to the wall by a very short piece of flex. This meant going on one's hands and knees to use the damn thing. Exasperated, I telephoned Stella.

This evening Stella and her kindly husband, Andreas, dropped by. While Andreas and Tim disappeared aloft to disconnect the answerphone, Thekla Junior and her small brother, Kyriakos, crashed about below. Snatching a box of matches from the latter and rescuing my Chinese 'Ming' horse from the clutches of the former, I managed to get both children's attention directed on to a spot of artwork. Their mother, tired from a day's work, looked on. While Kyriakos made careful patterns using one colour at a time, Thekla Junior – of the sharp pinches – made mud pies with all the colours, mixing them together and sloshing them across my expensive watercolour paper with gay abandon. Tim and Andreas came downstairs to report that the answerphone was more difficult to budge than they had imagined and they had therefore left it. Andreas and Stella departed after a round of Keo beer, their daughter's screams of protest at being removed from her artwork rending the air.

'She can come any time,' I called from the front doorstep and immediately regretted it. Seldom have I come across a more hyperactive three-year-old. The screaming continued as far as the car park, where the decibel levels dropped away as the family drove off.

'Isn't it a luxury to have a phone upstairs?' I said joyfully as Tim and I prepared to retire for the night. 'I'll just give Maria a buzz.'

I lifted the receiver.

A dead sound. A very dead sound.

Wednesday

Fed up with domestic difficulties, I decided to pay a call on Maria. Maria and her mother and sister are refugees from Famagusta, once a city of over three hundred churches and many other glories. The Greeks still call it Amochostos. Now it lies in the Turkish occupied north of the island and is but a shadow of its former self, its old buildings in ruins, its gracious gardens given over to weeds.

Maria and her sixteen cats live in the upper village. I marvel at her adaptability every time I visit her as her domestic hiccups with the locals rival my own. Once a New York dweller, she has taken a giant leap across the cultures, having converted some redundant houses in the old Turkish quarter of the village.

'When I came here, Leez, I had seven years living with the sheep. Everywhere, there were the sheep, so I write protest letters, I make telephone calls. They are coming into my house, these sheep. I send my compliments to the Minister of Agriculture. I go and see the Minister. Now, after seven years the sheep go. They are down there in the valley with the goats.'

46

Maria's house, her 'chicken coops' strung together so charmingly behind a wide verandah, reminds me of our country homesteads in Australia. She has done wonders with her garden, perched as it is at the head of the valley, on the edge of the village.

'It was the view. I told myself I can live with the dust and the neighbours. The view is enough.'

The neighbours have learned that Maria has not time to take coffee with them every day. She is an artist and must work. They have also learned that she has a front door which marks the boundary of her territory. She was obliged finally to lock it when a neighbour, kicking it open one day in her haste, dashed across the garden, leapt on to Maria's garden wall and bellowed at a distant figure tending the sheep.

'You can come now, mother. Lunch is ready!'

Maria's paintings are marvellously imaginative. I gazed at her wonderful designs – fish, angels, dragons, strange monsters, Grecian heads, phoenix-like birds of jewelled colours, mystic, dream-like.

Maria has opened a little shop next door to the hotel. We spent a hot afternoon there today, arranging its wooden sign low enough to catch the eye but high enough to escape the vehicles which squeeze their way along the narrow streets. The first sign, which Maria painted on an old piece of fencing, is not suitable. The lettering is too faint.

'It needs to stand out more. Catch the eye.'

'Yes, Leez, you are right.'

Inside the shop are arrayed items of pottery by local craftsmen in glazes of ultramarine and cerulean, colours of the Mediterranean; vases, candle holders, jewellery, 'Bronze Age and Neolithic' pottery figurines with their typically quaint troll-like faces and elongated necks. These Neolithic people, the first settlers of Cyprus, are said to have reared their babies with their heads placed in square boxes so that the heads come out a similar shape. Their settlements, approximately five thousand years BC, are still to be seen nearby at Khirokitia, the small round stone houses clustered together like the cells of a honeycomb.

At the end of our labours Maria and I, sticky with dust and heat, stood together in the lane and admired our window display. Some of Maria's paintings on glass had pride of place.

'I will call it The Gallery Shop,' said Maria.

Friday

The Cyprus Weekly is an excellent little English newspaper, read mostly, one imagines, by the expatriate. One article has taken my eye as it struck an encouraging note among so many sad reports about the north–south divide.

> This week something cheerful is going on in the 'mixed' village of Pyla in the UN controlled buffer zone. This village is a far cry, it seems, from the scenes of dereliction that are to be seen in much of Turkish Occupied Cyprus. One thousand two hundred Greek and Turkish Cypriots live in harmony here, as indeed they did in many villages before politics broke up the harmony. Pyla is the only mixed village left on the island. Recently the residents decided to beautify the village and to restore it, starting with a Turkish Cypriot Coffee Shop and a Greek Orthodox church. The United Nations High Commission for Refugees is funding the project.

Photographs of happy Cypriots mixing cement and digging holes appear in *The Cyprus Weekly* today. This project provides work for the locals and was the brainchild of the Turkish Cypriot mukhtar and his Greek Cypriot counterpart. When two young Greeks were murdered by Turkish troops last year, Turkish Cypriots working in the government-held areas lost their jobs. No one would employ them and their safety outside Pyla could not be guaranteed. The two mukhtars wrote to the United Nations and help arrived. Fourteen of the fifteen unemployed Turkish Cypriots are working on the coffee shop while ten Greek Cypriots are busy on the church. After that, attention will be directed to the village square.

The visitor to Pyla is greeted outside the village by the sign of a skull and crossbones. Old mines are in the area, to the right and left of the road. If the visitor continues on, however, he will see some encouraging things...

Tuesday

This morning I telephoned Thekla from the hotel. Very well, she will send Mr Stephanopolous back. She is very busy. Did I not know that today the school children are arriving? Busloads of them from all over the island! This week is the Week of the School Children. They are coming to explore the village and to eat at The House of the Wind. Thekla must press on. There is *klefiko* for the main course and always the popular *lookoomathes* for afters. Visions of the indefatigable Thekla juggling myriads of little doughnut balls in her cauldron of boiling oil spring to mind.

At 11 a.m. the son of Mr Stephanopolous arrived here, unannounced. He poked thoughtfully at both telephones and remarked that he is really a university student, not an electrician. He said he does not think that answerphones are common in Cyprus. Besides he has brought no tools with him, and so he left.

I got in the car and drove up the mountain. Thekla was in her kitchen peeling mountains of potatoes.

'Thekla, we simply have to have a telephone. It is in your name, you know. Please do something.'

'I can do nothing,' she wailed.' Mr Stephanopolous cannot come. It is the olive season.'

'What has that got to do with it?'

Thekla shot me a look of pity. 'He is picking the olives.'

But of course! How silly of me! What else would any self-respecting electrician be doing? 'How long will he be picking the olives?' I asked.

49

'For one month.'

Thekla's tone suggested any further questions would not only be supremely ignorant but futile.

'Have you asked the bank?' she asked suddenly, as she began an attack on a sack of onions. 'Maybe you paid your bill too late.' Her tone was dark.

At the Popular Bank George smiled broadly. Of course he will arrange direct debiting for all our future bills. A pity that Thekla had forgotten to forward us the last one.

A hearty voice interrupted my train of thought as I waited for George to do the paperwork.

'Ah. My friend Liz! How are you today?'

It is Doros, late of Birmingham but now home again and running his lace and silver shop.

'You know my friend Liz?' he boomed, attracting the attention of everyone, including the manager behind his glass screen. 'She is a lovely lady. I think that in her youth she must have been very beautiful!'

'I can believe that,' nodded George.

'Yes. That is true,' agreed Stavros, the second clerk, solemnly.

Without waiting to hear what the manager's contribution might be, I beat a hasty retreat.

Monday

My new Cyprus bank card has taken weeks to arrive. I have called at the bank half a dozen times. George will do his best to hurry it along.

I was somewhat taken aback this afternoon when a young man, half hidden behind a mountain of soft drink cans which he was unloading from a truck by the Tourists Café, called out, 'Have you got your bank card yet?'

Irritation that my private affairs were, apparently, becoming common knowledge in the village led me to reply rather curtly in the negative, until it dawned on me that the enquirer, emerging from behind the truck in an open-necked canary yellow shirt, was Stavros. Gone was his immaculate suit. It is quite usual for people here to have two jobs on the go. Last week, as a procession of marching school children, led by a pipe band, swung past Anna's hotel, I was ordered to remove my car by 'Post Office George', now smartly disguised in his role as part-time policeman and traffic warden. I was blocking the alleyway with my Mazda and celebrations to mark the Week of the School Children were still in progress.

Thursday

Tim is very pleased with his old Rover, which should be in a museum. I can hear him coming home a good fifteen minutes before he arrives. He has attached a suitably antique horn made of brass and rubber, found in a junk shop, by the driver's window and the Greek Cypriot flag and Union Jack to the mudguards. Maria and I were given a trial run to the next village and bounced about on its old springs until we begged for mercy. Meanwhile I am more than content with my 1990 Mazda, which hums along the empty roads like a summer bee. Japanese cars, second hand, are very common here, all at bargain prices. A young Cypriot friend from Nicosia helped us with its purchase as he knows an honest dealer in Limassol! So far the car and the dealer are living up to our hopes.

Monday

I am behind with my diary.

Roslyn has only just left us. She arrived one afternoon after what seemed like an unnecessarily complicated flight but I did not press her for details. Amongst her luggage was a giant-sized

51

suitcase of dried flowers from her extensive garden. They are most welcome at any time of year here, but especially in winter. One of her gardeners does the picking while Roz herself does the drying process. The flowers are hung in bunches upside down and are festooned along acres of hallways and in one large room at home, much to the irritation of husband, William.

'Libby, darling! I'm so happy in your dear little hotel! How clever of you to arrange it all for me! How are the dogs?'

We are sitting by the swimming pool, where Roz has persuaded the hard-pressed Soulla to serve her her breakfast on a tray. The morning sun fills the terrace and we luxuriate.

'The dogs are all right,' I begin. 'We're getting used to them as we've installed air conditioning and can shut our bedroom windows–'

But Roz isn't listening. She is examining her bare legs as we await her breakfast. Let's hope a week's sea bathing will help. There are nasty raw rashes spreading visibly. While she moves her gaze upwards to examine her arms, I hear all about the impossible Mavis. It seems that the poor woman is very stupid, knowing nothing of country ways. There are so many problems! Take lettuces, for instance. The situation has got so bad Roz is obliged to leave little notes about the kitchen. 'Mavis, would you please try to remember that Mr T likes the lettuces with the pink, crinkly edges' (pointless to give them their proper name!) 'and not the round ones? Do speak to Travers, the head gardener, if you are confused.' 'This is the knife for opening oysters. Do call me if you need help.' Or again, 'Could you try to remember these are the little forks for the lobster claws' etc. etc.

'I am in despair,' says Roz, as she piles a dollop of Anna's mother's home-made marmalade on to her toast. 'Michael is hardly speaking to me!'

Roz's eldest son, heir to the estate, is a genial fellow, not easily rumpled. However, it transpires that Mavis managed to ruin the roast pheasant last month – or was it grouse? – after a rather important shoot. Burnt black, it was! The humiliation of it all, what with the Lord Lieutenant of the County there, a baronet or two and old Colonel Nigel Woppington-Trump, second cousin to the Earl of B——.

As memories of this disastrous dinner party are still fresh in Roz's mind, I divert her thoughts with talk of our forthcoming dinner dance the following Saturday night. She brightens up immediately. Members of the Balkan Bar Association will be attending and Tim, as a lawyer, will be one of the hosts. Like her mother, my Aunt Eileen, whose intensely blue eyes and good looks she has inherited, Roz dearly loves a party.

While Roz munches through her fourth piece of toast, my thoughts wander back to the dear old Queensland days of my childhood and to Aunt Eileen making a cat's dinner out of trying to serve tea and scones to the occasional busload of tourists who managed to tear themselves away from the Sunshine Coast and go up to the mountains. Eileen spent thirty frustrated years on top of her mountain, while Uncle Tom made scones and tried to grow passion fruit as a commercial proposition. He had come to Australia as a young Englishman of devastating good looks and equally good connections but limited means and met my aunt in Brisbane at some flappers' party. Aunt Eileen did not relish life on the mountain but her three children ran about among the lush meadows and tropical rain forest, barefoot, free as air. Roz was obsessed with nature, particularly butterflies. I remember as a child watching with horrified fascination as she skewered their soft bodies on to display boards with dressmaker's pins.

Aunt Eileen, her children grown and fled, got to her Mecca at last. While Uncle Tom took a fishing rod and disappeared all day, Eileen drove herself about Sydney to avant-garde parties, concerts, art shows. She was still doing this well into her eighties, her form so shrunken now that her nose barely rose above her steering wheel. 'Oh, darling, isn't this fun!'

At the party for the Balkan Bar Association, her daughter became sweet sixteen again. Her magnificent eyes a-sparkle, a flame-coloured girdle tied 'ancient Greek-wise' about her expanding waist, my cousin threw herself into The Spirit of the Thing with her mother's gusto. The party was held at Anna's hotel, giving our Anna some good business as we near the end of the summer season. As 'Zorba the Greek' struck up from a corner, where a couple of musicians perspired gently from their exertions, Roz's come-hither glances attracted the attention of a Bulgarian lawyer whose enormous bulk took up more than his fair share of table space.

Rising heavily from his chair, he made his way across the floor and swept my cousin into a passionate, foot-stamping display at the end of a chain of dancers a good deal more youthful than themselves. When opportunity allowed, Roz would give a toss of her wavy hair and once or twice managed, with commendable dexterity, a quick lift of the hem of her skirt.

The following day Tim received a phone call at his office. The Bulgarian lawyer would like to know the name of the English lady in the yellow dress. In fact, he wished to take her out one night 'after 11 p.m.'

With commendable presence of mind, Tim fielded the invitation. Were there not several English ladies present? He was sorry, but he had no recollection of one in a yellow dress. He wasn't very observant . . .

Roz was crestfallen. 'Libby darling, why didn't you tell me?'

'Roz dear, we have probably saved you from a rather nasty experience. These Eastern Bloc types – drugs – Mafia – one never knows. A nice country girl like you!'

'I should have managed beautifully. I would have been nice – but firm.'

'Well, you might not have been nice enough. And then what?'

To distract her thoughts from an *Arabian Nights* opportunity missed, I suggested we took a day trip to Aphrodite's Temple. On reflection, this was probably not the most tactful of suggestions, but Roz was happy with any diversion. Off we went. The days of clear skies we had had for her first few days suddenly changed and dramatic pewter-coloured clouds accompanied us on our drive

55

along the coast. (Farmers and citrus growers are pinning their hopes on good rain after years of worsening conditions.) After an hour or so we reached our destination and parked the car just as a flash of lightning warned us to hurry. As we raced for the shelter of the museum, down came the welcoming rain, and at the foot of the steps in front of the medieval building, Roz tripped and fell flat on her face. Bravely she got to her feet and we reached shelter, half soaked. The museum, a large two storey structure, though open, was deserted.

We poked about among the ancient artefacts.

'Isn't this wonderful, darling? Just look at that bath tub! All carved in stone – let's see – over two thousand years ago! Oh look! There's even a plug hole and a ledge for the soap! Did they use soap, I wonder? And here's a head. Isn't she beautiful? And that great pointed stone. Do you suppose it's a phallic symbol or something?'

The ancient sanctuary outside dates from the late Bronze Age. As we studied the explanatory inscriptions beside each relic of Aphrodite's colourful 'reign', it became clear that this heavenly creature, born of the sea foam, beloved of artists from time immemorial, was indeed a bit of a gal. How to equate the lovely goddess with some of the goings on in and beyond her sanctuary became more difficult with each word we read. Originally worshipped as a goddess of war as well as of the sea, Aphrodite was finally demoted by the ancient Greeks. Homer reminds her in the *Iliad* that 'fighting, my child, is not for you. You are in charge of wedlock and the tender passions'. However, the cult of Aphrodite introduced into Cyprus prostitution 'as disgraceful', as one historian put it, 'as that practised by the women of Babylon'. Perhaps not surprisingly, the local populace were said to be 'the happiest beings on earth', some, perhaps, happier than others.

Cyprus was rich in many things, from its vast timber forests, its grain, hemp and flax, its dyes from plants such as henna, but above all from its copper mines, and the luxury enjoyed by the nobility, in particular, led to the worship of Aphrodite going overboard, so to speak. Finally, in disgust, the Emperor Justinian closed all pagan temples throughout the Roman empire and brought the worship of Aphrodite to an official end. However, this move was ignored by the Cypriots for centuries to come. During the visit of Paul and Barnabas to the island pagan sanctuaries were still being built.

'You really begin to believe in her, don't you? I mean, you feel she was *real.*'

Another flash of lightning at this point brought us both to our senses. A crack of thunder following it was so violent that the ancient rafters above us shook. Out went all the lights. We stood together in the semi-darkness.

'Aphrodite speaks!' giggled Roz.

Wednesday

There has been no sign whatever of Sophocles' municipal truck. The grapes which the old folk could have enjoyed are rotting on our vine and the wasps are in seventh heaven.

Friday

Roz's dried flowers have filled in many empty spaces, especially in the sitting room.

Our week at Pissouri beach, in a rented flat, has had a certain therapeutic benefit on her legs. The eczema has eased off. My cousin was quite undeterred by the temperature of the water and plunged merrily into the waves, where she bobbed about for sixty minutes at a stretch. I remained firmly on dry land. By the time Tim and I had seen her off at the airport we felt she was well on the way to coping with the vicissitudes of life with Cook.

NOVEMBER

Monday

'We've got to be really firm with Thekla this time,' I said to Tim. 'I've made out a list of things we want done. More than half a dozen, at least.'

'Right,' said Tim.

Thekla arrived forty minutes late. Monday is her least busy day, she says. She was in her smart patterned dress with her gold 'antique' earrings. She wore elegant black court shoes. How does she get the time, I wondered: time to change and do her hair and look so nice? We exchanged '*kalisperas*' and Tim offered her a drink.

'I cannot,' she laughed mournfully, 'I must work.'

She accepted a fruit juice and we settled together on the hard little couch in the front parlour. Tim stood coyly in the kitchen doorway. Taking a gulp of the local vodka, I began gently but firmly.

'Now, Thekla. You know we have been in your house for some months. When can you give us a chest of drawers? The one that belonged to your mother has drawers that stick and go sideways when you open them. Besides, we do badly need one other.'

'But how can I give you more furniture? If I buy more furniture I pay too much!'

I did not mean to be tactless about her mother's furniture. Together with an old carved wardrobe and a giant-sized mirror hanging on a pair of meat hooks in the spare room, it makes up the family collection of heirlooms. All these pieces have been covered in many layers of chocolate-coloured paint and are rife with history.

'Yes, but we are paying you rent,' I suggested carefully.

'What shall I do? My daughter, we pay for her house! My feet. Look at my ankles!'

They were indeed painfully swollen.

'My condition. I cannot drink alcohol. It is very bad.'

Things were beginning to wander off course. I left the subject of furniture and tried another tack. Tim was being unhelpful in his corner.

'The gas griller. It does not work.'

'What can I do? The other lady who was here before you, she bought the cooker.'

'She bought it?'

'Yes, of course. I do not know anything about it.'

'In that case, could you tell us of someone who can mend it? It is difficult to find people around here.'

'You must get someone yourself,' Thekla replied, unhelpfully. 'I cannot do it. I have too much work. Yesterday, Tassos and I, we are working from eight o'clock in the morning until two o'clock last night. My legs! I cannot sleep with the pain!'

We nodded sympathetically. Had she tried soluble aspirin?

'It is very hard.'

'Yes,' we agreed. We were very sorry.

'The son of the mukhtar, he will mend your grill,' Thekla volunteered.

Cheered by this small step, I made a note of this. Chrisso, the charming wife of the mukhtar, speaks a little English. I will ask her.

'About the hot water. There is no longer hot water in the morning. Do we have to wait for the sun to heat it up?'

'You must turn on the switch! Plenty of hot water. You do not wait for the sun!'

With surprising agility for someone with sore feet, Thekla leapt from her seat and jerking back one of the parlour curtains revealed the mystery item.

Tim and I exchanged foolish glances. Our house has its water tank and solar panels on the roof, as do all the island's houses. Now, cool air is blowing from the mountains and nature needs a helping hand. I felt it was Tim's job to know about booster switches – we agreed with Thekla it was very silly of us.

'There is also the problem with the wood-burning stove,' Tim began, to change the subject. 'It has a pane of glass missing. We will need to use it soon.'

Thekla examined the stove critically.

'The other lady, she puts it here. It was good when it was in the kitchen. But you have no need of a piece of glass! Look! I always leave the door open. It is good.'

But for once I was on strong ground. I have grown up with wood-burning stoves. A missing pane affects the efficiency of the thing, I pointed out. Besides, it will smoke.

'OK. I will send Tassos.'

(Aye, but will he come?)

I scanned through our list. Most urgent, of course, is the leaking chimney pipe upstairs. There is also the problem of the kitchen cupboards, or rather the cupboard doors. They keep falling off. Whenever Tim screws them back, in no time at all they spit their screws all over the floor. No doubt these cupboards are the responsibility of the other lady? Has she been responsible for the whole kitchen, tiles and all? She has put up some useful shelves, too, on which repose our knick knacks from home and our Moroccan teapot, all set off by Thekla's icon of St Michael. Altogether it is a charming kitchen, thanks to the efforts of 'the other lady', the previous tenant.

'Have you finished with the iron?' Thekla asked suddenly. She pronounced the word as I-ron and for a moment I was nonplussed.

'Oh, do you want it back just yet? Our goods are coming by sea and they won't be here for a few more weeks.'

'My son, Chris, he needs me to I-ron for him. Very quickly. I must get up at five o'clock to do it. He has new job. He must work hard. He is getting married in two years. My I-ron takes too long to get hot. I am standing too much. My foot! Here. Look at my foot!'

Thekla removed the Marks and Spencer shoe on her right foot. Her second toe had a nasty look. It was drawn up, so that a large bunion had grown on the first joint.

60

'My doctor, he says I must go and have an operation but I am frightened to go.'

From the dim and distant past, I remembered some of my occupational therapy medical training.

'What about a splint for it?' I suggested. 'You could make a comfy splint for your toe with sticking plaster. You have developed what is called a hammer toe,' I concluded, rather pleased with my diagnosis.

Thekla had not heard.

'My children. They do not want to do all this work. It is too much. All day and all night we are working! Some people they come yesterday. They order one bowl of salad and two forks! I make two pounds profit only on each person who eats at our restaurant.'

'You're a wonderful woman!' I told her.

'Can't you put your prices up?' Tim suggested.

'No. The people, they will go somewhere else.'

'Even by fifty cents?' he added.

'The government tells us what we must charge. Now they send the Health Inspector! He tells us we must make a bigger kitchen! He says it is not healthy. It is very hard.'

I agreed to return Thekla's iron next week. Clearly her problems are mind-blowing compared to ours.

'Take care!' we called after her retreating figure.

Game, set and match to the patroness of The House of the Wind.'

I wrote to my elderly mother regularly, as her apprehension about her daughter living far away on an island in a politically sensitive area of the Mediterranean needed lessening with accounts of our everyday life. However, perhaps the following letter was not as tactful as it might have been.

Evagora has been weeping for days, even weeks. You will

remember she is our immediate neighbour. Her beloved Achilles is to go into the Army in a few months' time. Achilles, her third son, is as beautiful as Adonis. On Saturday evenings he dresses up in his smartest clothes and goes off to the bright lights down on the coast. His dark hair is glued to his head with gel like a modern-day Rudolph Valentino: his favourite shirt is a shiny lime-green. I defy any film producer to pass him by without a second glance.

'The Army, it does terrible things to these boys,' Evagora wails. 'Twenty-six months they must spend there! The food is terrible. We have to take them food when we can. And the clothes they must have! It's very expensive for us, but what does the Army care? What does it care about twenty-six months taken out of a young man's life? And sometimes there are terrible accidents! I can't bear to think about it.'

Cyprus is one of the most heavily and densely garrisoned countries on earth. Last week I visited my favourite art shop in Nicosia. It was closed for the day. The nice man who sells me materials had gone into the Army for the day. Before that our village post office was closed one weekday. Michaelis and George had gone! Another day George at the bank was away. These are the older men. My doctor complains bitterly about the compulsory two weeks a year he must do. How can he leave his patients? But the young men have the worst deal. Those Adonis-like young men bronzing themselves on your Sydney beaches have no idea how fortunate they are.

All love

Libby

Thursday

Today a short piece appeared in *The Cyprus Weekly*. 'PROPHET ELIJAH LIFTED MY SHED' read the headline, and underneath a photograph of the tangled remains of the said building, lying on a grassy hillside.

'In the village of K— the talk is all about miracles,' said the article.

Yes, our village has seen a miracle! It was witnessed by a resident out picking mushrooms and also by the owner of the shed himself. The latter told reporters that the Prophet had lifted his two-ton building six metres off the ground and hurled it fifty metres downhill. It landed near the foundations of an uncompleted chapel which the shed owner has been dilatory in completing. The chapel is to be dedicated to the memory of his son. The Prophet was giving the shed owner a timely reminder of where his priorities should lie, our village priest endorsing the warning.

This afternoon Old Crystalla, Maroulla and I sat in our usual places under the former's grapevine. Maroulla is Crystalla's daughter. The vine leaves are now falling as winter approaches. Producing a dish of her father's corn cobs, Maroulla explained why her mother's house was empty the day Tim and I called on her last week. It is very rare not to find the old lady at home.

'My mother and I, we go to Trachori,' Maroulla told us.

'Is that near here?'

'It is near Limassol. We saw the miracles.' Maroulla (instead of Maria, we now call her by her pet name) allowed her voice to drop.

Crystalla's usually smiling face looked very solemn. Mother and daughter went to a small house not far from the sea. Many people were there and it wasn't easy to enter. In fact, the owner of the house had had to move out! In each room a cross has appeared. A cross on each wall, and on one wall there has come a face. The face was round, pale yellow, like the corn on the table where we sat, Maroulla explained, pointing to one of her father's cobs. She had touched the image, but not on the face, of course.

'I touch near it, on the wall.'

Behind her thick glasses Crystalla let the tears fall.

'It was very wonderful. My mother and I, we cry.'

'*Ne. Ne,*' nodded the old lady. That is true.

We sat in silence for a while. Then Maroulla, brightening suddenly, asked, 'Mr Timotheos? He likes the donkey?'

'Oh yes,' I fibbed. In truth, Tim has been nowhere near Madonna these last three months. Work is his excuse. Too much work. Instead, it is left to me to save Madonna extra-large carrots and to give her a good brushing with a curry comb when the spirit moves me. This latter action, in particular, comes as a pleasurable surprise to Madonna, unused as she is to such treatment whether out in the fields or in her yard. She stands to attention, her neat little hooves four square, her Elizabeth Taylor eyelashes drooping on heavy lids. After a while her head droops as well. 'Oh don't stop, please,' she tells me.

'Good,' laughed Maroulla. 'I will tell my brother. Agamemnon will be very happy Mr Timotheos he likes the donkey.'

Friday

Yesterday our furniture arrived from Sydney. What a joy to see our pictures and books, nothing smashed as far as we can tell. My painting of the Opera House looks fine in the kitchen and the little statue of Rodin's *Kiss* has gone on one of the deep window sills of the sitting room, as has our ornate green and white Italian jug. Our three Persian rugs have 'gentrified' the grey tiled floor here. I must wait patiently for Tim to help me hang the other paintings. The gilt-framed Filipino looking glass will give a dash of Spanish antiquity to our front parlour. Fortunately Thekla has provided acres of spare shelves for books.

DECEMBER

Saturday

My five Australian cousins have just left us, our second lot of guests. Three of them were parked at Anna's hotel, there not being enough space in our little house. They had been advised by their travel agent in Brisbane that there were no direct flights from the United Kingdom to Cyprus! They thus got up well before dawn at their English address, travelled all day and waited six hours in Athens, 'an airport to be avoided at all costs'. A journey which should have taken four and a half hours from Gatwick Airport had been more than trebled. However, their spirits soon revived.

Lawrie borrowed my copy of *The Fall of Constantinople*. Time being short, he started at 'the rape and pillage bit'. He said he had always wanted to get to grips with Byzantium and was taking his family to Turkey for Christmas. Direct flights from Greek Cypriot Cyprus to Turkey are forbidden but another diversion back via Athens did not seem to daunt him. A charming quiet fellow whose family of teenagers use him as their butt for all jokes, Lawrie spent awestruck moments in our little chapel of Ayios Michaelis up by the car park. Here the sombre faces of the saints gaze, El Greco-like, from the wall of the apse behind the tiny altar. Frescoes of a later date in the main part of the chapel glimmer dimly from the ageing plaster. The Bishop of Limassol was banished here in 1222. How did the bishop adapt to such a tiny congregation, for the church can hold barely two dozen worshippers? A very big fish in a very small pond, he must have filled the local people with as much awe as the sombre-faced saints gazing down from their places on the dimly lit walls.

Richard, aged nineteen, decided to concentrate on the Third Crusade and on his namesake, Richard the Lionheart. He discovered that the latter was blown to Cyprus in a storm in 1192 when on his way to the Holy Land. Richard had his fiancée, Berengaria, with him but she travelled in a different ship and was unfortunate enough to reach the Cyprus shore ahead of her future husband. Isaac, King of Cyprus, was unwise enough to rob and imprison some of the crew. This act effectively ended forever Byzantine rule on the island. Richard defeated Isaac in several short sharp battles, following up his victories with his wedding in Limassol. Perhaps it was at this wedding that he grew to appreciate the island's fine wines for he is reputed to have said later that to taste these again would be reason enough to return.

King Richard's hold on Cyprus lasted but a few weeks, as he was in a hurry to join the Crusades. He soon found a ready buyer for the island in the Knights Templar, a greedy bunch, who paid him forty thousand bezants for it, with a promise of a further sixty thousand bezants to come. The Knights were soon forced out of the island after several bloody uprisings, the local population growing tired of their exceeding cruelty. While unable to repay Richard the sixty thousand bezants still owed to him, they gave one gift to Cyprus, their sweet Commandaria wine made in their Grand Commandery at Kolossi Castle. Richard then resold the island to the dispossessed King of Jerusalem, Guy de Lusignan, one of his henchmen. This French family ruled Cyprus for the next three hundred years.

Cousin Tom, aged fourteen, took up the research here. Greek property owners and nobles on the island having been virtually wiped out by the brutal reign of the Knights Templar, Guy de Lusignan 'sent forth tidings to all surrounding countries that all knights, nobles and citizens desirous of fiefs and land' should come to Cyprus. 'Thus they came from the Kingdom of Jerusalem, from Tripoli, from Antioch and Armenia. Many were from the lower classes and included non-Cypriot Greeks.'

Conflict between the Roman Catholic and Greek Orthodox Churches escalated, the de Lusignans being, of course, members of the Catholic faith. Greek bishoprics were reduced to four and these were in remote villages, while their bishops were forced to swear an oath of loyalty. (Thirteen Greek Orthodox monks had been burnt at the stake by a Dominican padre in 1231.) While the indigenous church fared badly under Lusignan rule, a German pilgrim travelling through the country in the fourteenth century reported the princes, nobles and knights to be 'the wealthiest in the world'. He also commented on the cult worship of Aphrodite, still flourishing centuries after her banishment, and in particular on the prostitution in the temple at Paphos.

To add to this confusing picture, Genoa and Venice had their own independent rival states within Cyprus. One of the Lusignan Kings, Peter II, was thrown from his throne in the very act of his coronation and for the next ninety years the Genoese occupied Famagusta. They were soon followed by the Venetians, who took over the whole island and ruled it from 1489–1570. In July of that year three hundred and fifty Turkish ships landed at Larnaca and the island fell. The Greeks fought bravely on the side of their Venetian rulers, who held out for a further ten months in Famagusta. As conversion to Islam was a pre-condition for the Venetians to remain on the island, there was a catastrophic drop in the population; some fled, while many islanders died in a series of natural disasters, earthquakes being one of them.

The Moslems allowed the Christians a certain amount of self-government, however, and the pattern of Christians and Moslems living alongside one another, but in separate areas of towns and villages, was established. All in all, the Greek Cypriot preferred the change from Venetian Roman Catholic rule to Ottoman rule. The power of the Greek Orthodox Church was renewed and monasteries flourished, but the monks became greedy and the Church joined the Ottomans in corrupt government. The Greeks on the island became better educated and prospered, while the Turkish population grew poorer.

British troops arrived on the island in 1878 and it fell to British rule. In 1881 the census reported 140,793 Greek Cypriots and 42,638 Turkish Cypriots to be living on Cyprus. While the British introduced a more liberal system of government, they regarded the island as a strategic base, first and foremost. There was very little investment and much indigenous poverty.

Tom and Richard did their research well and enlightened us.

Tim and I were not the only ones sorry to say goodbye to my Australian cousins, who had combed the island with a fine tooth comb in their eagerness to explore. Evagora's handsome sons, Marcos and Achilles, cast wistful eyes at the departing figure of eighteen-year-old Christina. The three young Australians did not allow the language barrier to get in their way and spent jolly evenings next door, all squashed into the tiny front parlour like sardines. Evagora went to and fro from her kitchen plying the company with platefuls of *kourambiedes,* little Christmas cookies dusted with icing sugar.

Wednesday

'Why do the village people call you Liz?' Tim asked today.

'I suppose its because Evagora suggested it and I agreed. Apparently "Libby" in Greek means "sad"! I quite like it, don't you?'

'I expect I will when I get used to it.'

Friday

A sack of oranges was waiting for us on our doorstep when we got home today. I suspect they are from Michaelis or Takis. The latter sits on his special chair under 'the tree of idleness' most days. But he is not idle. When not working on his orchard, cutting firewood, tending his hens etc., he is busying himself with trimming twigs to make into brooms. We have one of these brooms for the courtyard. The handle is cut from oleanders, the twiggy bits come from a bush 'that grows by the little river'. Takis himself has his chair with its position clearly delineated thus:

'TAKIS. HIS REST PLACE', the letters scratched out on the stone wall behind.

The oranges are deliciously sweet, much sweeter than the ones I bought from Father S, who came hawking his produce not long ago and to whom I gave one pound. While the higher clergy live well, as do those in the numerous monasteries, the lowly village priest must supplement his income by cultivating the family plot and selling the produce. No doubt our priest's wife is expected to add lace making to her many chores.

According to a lecture we attended in Nicosia recently, it is the citrus growers who are hogging more than their fair share of water on the island. They use up far more than some of the tourists on the coast, in spite of the daily changes of clean hotel linen and the green hotel lawns on which the tourists may spread their suntanned bodies. As we munched our oranges, the sobering thought came to us that perhaps, one day soon, the oranges of Cyprus (and the lemons and the limes) will be a luxury that the island can no longer afford to produce.

Dearest Ma,

Christmas has come and gone but it was not like Christmas at all, of course. The sun still shines warmly, the vine is still loaded with grapes, but you are all absent. Tim has hung a garland of holly on our front door. I made an extra Christmas pudding (your recipe) for Evagora, Andreas and the four boys, plus Evagora's mother, Myafora. I only hope the pudding went round. The male members of the family are very large. The brandy butter, I explained, was an essential extra. In exchange, Evagora brought over a plate of her tasty *kourambiedes*. As Chrisso, the mukhtar's wife, has also plied us with samples of her baking, as has Androulla down the lane, we have enough to feed an army. Androulla, another neighbour, speaks no English but her friendly generosity is ever-present.

69

'Silver Chris' and his English-Cypriot wife, Linda, very kindly invited us for Christmas lunch. Chris, the silversmith, lit a cheerful barbecue in his yard and the lunch table groaned with meats and salads, pastries and cakes, including the local Christmas cake dusted with sesame seeds and almonds. A positive bevy of cousins, aunts and uncles, grandparents and children were so closely packed that we sat like chickens with clipped wings. The weather allowed the overflow of guests to move to the yard when the crush became unbearable. Tim and I returned home in mid-afternoon, neither of us able to match the Cypriot appetite and wishing we had had the courage to say no earlier.

In spite of delicious food shared in good company, a sense of loss stayed with me for the rest of the day. At this special time of year these people are with their families. They are at home in their surroundings, while Tim and I, as yet, are beginners, just dipping our toes into this new life and sadly inept with the language.

NB Christmas Dish
Loin of pork marinated in red wine and ground coriander and then slowly smoked in a clay oven. I doubt you can get clay ovens in Sydney!

All love

Libby

Thursday

My nephew Clive arrived from Glasgow yesterday, beaming with delight as, under a sharp and starry sky, we two walked down the lane to our house. The heady smell of wood smoke drifted out from our log fire and mingled with the clear night air.

'Just the holiday I need!' he commented happily.

In spite of its broken pane – (No, Tassos did not come. As with 'spirits from the vasty deep', Thekla and Owen Glendower have uncertain control over such matters. In dealings with her husband, Thekla, like most Cypriot wives, bows to his superior will) – in spite of the broken pane, our wood stove is working tolerably well. When the wind is in the north and its smoke starts to fill the little parlour, Tim fixes a piece of kitchen foil over the gap.

Yesterday morning early, as Evagora and I swept winter leaves from our laneway, she informed me that Father S, the priest, wished to call on us.

'When?' I asked, somewhat aghast.

'This morning, I expect.'

'Oh dear. Tim is out. What will I give him?'

'Just Cyprus coffee. That's good enough,' she answered carelessly. She was in a hurry to get her washing pinned out. She promised that she would return to act as interpreter when the time came.

Evagora's washing, weather permitting, is a daily production line of five outfits of jungle greens, socks and underwear, her own items decorating the main arrangement like lace on a bedspread. To reach her washing lines she must mount a precarious ladder from one roof surface to another. The bowl of heavy washing is clasped under one arm while she grasps the ladder with the other. Convinced that one day the whole thing will end in disaster, I have urged her to get one of her strapping sons to build her some steps. But no, she assures me sadly, such refinements are not considered necessary household aids. Cypriot housewives are never coddled.

An hour or so later, with Clive still abed and Tim still not back from shopping, Father S swept through the front door, his waist-length grizzled beard preceding him, his tall black form hiding Evagora's small black figure in the rear. His intimidating priest's hat had been left at home, an omission for which I was thankful. Evagora instructed me in how much Cyprus coffee to put in our little one-man pot and then, to my dismay, bustled off. Some pressing matter to do with Marcos' goats, she said.

71

Father S and I stood awkwardly together in the parlour. From amongst the mass of bristling hair, a pair of remarkably youthful eyes looked out. The silence grew oppressive. I offered a digestive biscuit which was declined. I was thankful the coffee cup was small and its contents meagre. As Father S sipped his beverage, I began to edge myself carefully sideways until I had managed to obliterate my photograph of the Pope. This was not the time to stir up unfriendly ghosts, I felt. At last, the coffee finished, Father S handed back his cup and then suddenly, with alarming swiftness, leant towards me, planting a kiss firmly on both cheeks. A moment later, in a flurry of robes and jangling keys, he was gone!

'Who was that?' asked Clive sleepily, coming downstairs in his dressing gown.

'Um – er – only the priest,' I muttered.

JANUARY

Wednesday

The new year has brought two heavy storms this week, rolling in from the north. From the chill of the wind, they must have come from the snowfields of Turkey. The village people are delighted. The rain sweeps upon us, a great curtain of water, urged on by the ferocious winds. In seconds a positive cataract is rushing down our lane, almost deep enough to top our front doorstep and flood the parlour. It is a thrilling and gratifying sight, all this water. On it goes, past our house, round the corner and down the lane past Old Demetri and Crystalla. Here it does another right-angled turn and careers madly on past Demetri's fowl yard and orchard and down through his thirsty fields towards the dog pens. Soon, of course, it runs out of steam, so parched is the land. The desiccated fennel, the figs, almonds, carobs and lemon trees grasp hungrily with their roots. There can never be enough rain! Accompanying all this is the thrilling boom of the thunder, interspersed with the lightning flashes zigzagging and cracking over our heads as the eye of the storm passes and then grumbles away over the mountains. Only in Australia and Africa have I known storms like these. Long may they continue. There has been one casualty, however: our smart new doormat, a green one made of rubber, swept off on the tide. If a neighbour has not already grabbed it, it must be halfway down the valley by now.

Thursday

During the storm that raged yesterday, I went into our spare room to check our 'hanging' chimney pipe. The previous lodger, 'the other lady', must have left it like this when she moved the wood-burning stove from the kitchen below into the front parlour. The open end of the pipe is directly above Thekla's mother's wardrobe and in heavy rain it drips. It is surprising that this situation does not seem to concern our landlady, the said wardrobe being her family's heirloom. However, if Thekla does not mind about damage to her heirlooms, I at least mind about damage to my best silk blouse. At a party in Nicosia last week I noticed too late a dark brown stain down one of the sleeves.

It must be three months since we first mentioned the dripping pipe to Tassos. Tim has put our green plastic bucket on the top of the wardrobe as a temporary measure. He is not, alas, a do-it-yourself type. The bucket looks quite fetching as its green colour matches the bamboo shoots on the spare room's Chinese lampshade. Yesterday, when I went to check the water level in the bucket, soft pinging sounds greeted me. Small hail stones were bouncing out of the bucket on to the floor.

We had not imagined Cyprus having cold winters, but up here in the hills we are surprised by this. However, our three new air conditioners are dual-purpose, so to speak, and in seconds we have wonderful warm air blowing into the kitchen, bedroom and sitting room. Bit by bit Thekla's tenants are modernizing her house for her.

Monday

Would Greek lessons be in order?

Yesterday, as I sat in Crystalla's kitchen with the old lady and Androulla, her neighbour, our conversation wandered over various topics. We sat around the kitchen table beneath a 1920s betrothal portrait of our hostess and her husband, both of them wearing expressions that would have been more suitable at a wake. The young couple, looking old beyond their years, gaze fixedly ahead in mute obedience to the camera. Both appear to be wearing black but, if not black, certainly their Sunday best. Crystalla is without her thick spectacles and Demetri without his twinkling eyes. They stare down into a kitchen in which the only concession to modernity has been the addition of a small refrigerator and a calor gas stove. Off the courtyard outside are the two bedrooms in which six children were raised. One suspects that there is now also a bathroom. A well stands in the centre of the courtyard and is still very useful; the couple are fortunate to own a spring. The courtyard, a good deal larger than the house, is its prettiest 'room' and bright with tubs of geraniums and twining jasmine. Under a grape trellis are a table and chairs in constant use. Next door is the orchard and the fowl yard, the occupants a cheerful lot in their free-range roamings. The five white doves live under the eaves. From the grape trellis stretches the same view that Tim and I enjoy nearby, the shades of burnt siennas, dark or olive greens, tawny ochres and varying blues. In the centre of the far picture is the narrow strip of silver sea.

Old Crystalla and Demetri are both eighty-six and share the same birthday. Life for them, once of ceaseless grinding toil, finds them now with time to spend. Demetri chooses the coffee house for idle moments, while Crystalla sits beneath her grapevine and chats to the neighbours.

Firstly Crystalla, Androulla and I discussed our children and grandchildren, a good deal of finger work helping with numbers. One of Crystalla's five sons lives in Los Angeles. The rest seem to have stayed at home, as has the adored daughter, Maroulla. I think there are fifteen grandchildren. The good-natured Androulla has five sons and two daughters; her bachelor son assists Father S at Sunday services. She appears to have five grandchildren, one of whom has registered herself on my consciousness with her piercing shrieks as she plays beneath our window during my Sunday afternoon siestas.

I took out a pad and did a few rough sketches of my offspring, the action causing much mirth. Then I enquired after Madonna, not having visited her for some weeks, due to my touch of winter bronchitis. Yes, Madonna, she is well. She has had a little one, in fact. Old Crystalla's hand movements were very graphic.

'A little one?' I gasped. 'How wonderful!'

'*Ne. Ne.*' Crystalla beamed, her eyes as round as marbles behind her thick glasses.

Androulla beamed also. Allowing this news to sink in, the old lady passed round a delicious sweet made from locally ground almonds mixed with honey. We ate it on little dishes with spoons.

I must visit Madonna as soon as possible. Madonna, with her foal, will bring the donkey count in the village to five. Strange that I had not guessed her condition, but winter does seem an unsuitable time for giving birth. Next I enquired after Demetri.

The old lady's face fell. Ah. Demetri. He is in Larnaca. In hospital.

'In *hospital?*' I ask, incredulous. Demetri, of all people, ill?

Ne. Ne. He has gone to Larnaca with Maroulla. His stomach (here old Crystalla rubbed the black dress above her own) it is very bad.

'How did that happen?'

The answer is simple: *Limoni.* It transpires that Demetri had made the mistake of imbibing some lemonade at the mukhtar's coffee house. Clearly he should have stuck to something less dangerous. *Ne. Ne.* It was the *limoni* that did it. He has gone to hospital. Visions of stomach pumps, barium meals, gastric ulcers all sprang to mind. It is too sad. Demetri, so upright, such an active octogenarian! Demetri the donkey rider! I went home to tell Tim.

This morning I was up early and from the terrace I peered down the valley. Beyond the almond and carob trees, I could just make out the form of a happy mother donkey munching her breakfast. I put on trousers, long socks and boots and went off to investigate. My sudden appearance set Demetri's hens clucking and Crystalla's white doves flying. Not wanting to alarm the dogs in their kennels, I moved cautiously through the long grass to where Madonna had carved herself a 'corn circle' among the burgeoning fennel. Madonna, expecting carrots, gave a happy nicker and trotted forwards, but her tethering rope prevented her progress. There she was, in the pink as usual, but no baby donkey was to be seen. I poked around in the tall grass just to check the point. Madonna stuck her nose in my pocket. I gave her three carrots. 'You old fraud,' I told her.

This afternoon, by the church, I met Demetri! We stopped to exchange brief greetings, the old man's face creased with smiles as usual. Clearly he was on his way home from the coffee house. Never had a gastric ulcer looked in better fettle.

There is an evening class in Greek in Larnaca on Wednesdays. Should I enrol? I recall Xenios' advice.

Thursday

This is good walking weather. In the afternoons, taking the road that winds up towards the village of B—, the light changes moment by moment. With a painter's eye I work out how I would put in that mountainside ahead – cadmium yellow and black to make a nice mud green for the forests, burnt sienna toned with umber to suggest that favourite spur over there, ultramarine mixed with a touch of vermilion for those pockets of deep shadow, pale cobalt softening to cerulean for the sky. Small migratory birds are tinkling in the sclerophyllous scrub and broom. The silence is almost deafening, save for my plodding feet. Why then, today, do I feel so irritated?

Ahead, at a favourite bend in the road where a local Cypriot has his family plot, I spy another ugly building going up. Yet again, I note, another bunch of hens or clutch of pigs (or goats?) are about to be ushered into the front row of the stalls. If not the stalls, then the dress circle. What perversity of the Cypriot mind causes the locals to plant their animal pens on the very top of mountain spurs which have views lovely enough to make one faint? Considering their attitude to livestock, it is very puzzling. Today I note that the new shed, with its corrugated iron roof, has been placed next to its neighbour, the only difference in the two buildings being that this new shed has a small yard in front, a sort of viewing gallery for the occupants. The owner of this plot has tucked his pretty things, his fig trees and his vines, into a pocket of the hill nearby, as far out of sight as possible. The engine that pumps his irrigation water hums in its breeze block shed close to. The water comes from a spring below ground, the life blood of the little property. Down one side of the mountain spur on which the aforementioned sheds stand so proudly, catching the rays of the lowering sun, lies the rubbish tip. Down, down slide the plastic bags, the bottles, tin cans and pots, the rusting iron furniture, the old mattress from Great Grandmother's bed etc., etc. Like confetti is this rubbish, some of it sticking on to bushes, the odd blue plastic bag hanging flag-like from a protruding twig. One wonders if the livestock belonging to this Lord of the Manor do not have their sensibilities severely dented every time they turn their heads to the right. If not, why do the sad monks in the monastery on their high pinnacle yonder never object? Or do they too throw their rubbish down the hills? If so, it is too far off to spot from this particular bend in the road.

So high is this pinnacle on which the monastery is set, that it may be seen from vast distances, provided a mountain range does not intrude here and there. A score of monks call it home but it would be hard to visualize a place less homely with its dour setting and unwelcoming portals. During my nephew Clive's brief visit at New Year I drove him up the winding road to the monastery. A short sharp notice on the gate informs the visitor that no females are welcome and this includes entrance to the chapel which stands nearby. Before the road was built, an endless procession of patient donkeys, even camels, must have toiled with supplies up these stony slopes. The views are vast, yet the sea seems close, so high is the peak.

Clive had left me at the car and plodded, without too much enthusiasm, towards the monastery building, a thing of extraordinary ugliness. Not a single architectural embellishment adorns its outer walls, so that it has all the appearance of a prison block. A brief encounter with an elderly inhabitant persuaded Clive that today was perhaps not the best of days for a quick look round. We returned homewards, Clive a little shaken by the chill of his reception. 'So un-Christian,' he murmured, 'and so chauvinistic!'

'Yes, and to think that the place was founded by a woman!'

Monday

'And good morning. How are you?'

I am in the post office, collecting our mail. A portly gentleman standing by the counter extends his hand in greeting. He is wearing a tweed jacket and English-type tweed cap. I can remember a brief meeting last year but I cannot recall his name.

'My name is Achilles Andreou. I have just returned from London.' He beams at me through very thick spectacles.

'How nice. Was it cold?'

'Yes. It was very, very cold. I have been staying with my partner, so the cold, it did not concern me.'

A hoot of good-natured mirth from George, who is sorting the mail, greets this remark. Fortunately, our friend does not seem to notice.

'At the age of sixty-eight I have fallen in love,' he continues.

'I'm so glad. Is she a Cypriot?'

'She is more than half Cypriot. She speaks very good English,' replies my companion. 'She has also a very nice house, so I am much in love with her. London is very expensive.'

A fresh burst of suppressed merriment from George, this time joined by Michaelis. For some weeks the latter has not worn his usual genial expression and one day last week, when I arrived to fetch the mail, I found the post office closed. Michaelis' father-in-law had died. Today his elderly customer is providing some welcome light relief.

As I leave I recall the conversation last year. On that occasion, without any preliminaries, my friend of the tweed cap had approached me thus.

'You are English? Ah. I have something to ask you.'

'Yes?'

'Can you help me find a wife?'

'A wife?'

'Yes. I would like a wife but she must be English. Cypriot women are not satisfactory. Do you know an English woman?'

I replied that I would have to think about it and we parted. Happily, a more-than-half-Cypriot woman will now do.

There was one occasion during our Cypriot sojourn when our landlady's husband did stir himself on our behalf. The dripping chimney had been dripping for a very long time.

Tuesday

Carrying some shopping down our lane today, I noticed a ladder propped against our front wall. A familiar-looking truck was all but blocking my passage and the figure of Tassos was coming down the ladder. It waved an arm skywards in an abandoned manner.

'Look!' (So he does speak some English!)

There, on top of our chimney stack, was a red plastic bucket.

'How long is *that* going to last?' I asked as we both gazed upwards at the object in question.

'Maybe it stay one month. Maybe one year. Maybe two. Then maybe it blows away!'

Pleased with both his witticism and his efforts, Tassos drove off, a broad grin on his face. I stifled my irritation by reminding myself that he had at least given us a new shower attachment in the bathroom, thereby quelling a downstairs leak if not an upstairs one.

Wednesday

In spurts and starts, winter has set in. As I left the home of Old Kemon and Maria well muffled in my woollies, a great yellow moon, almost full, was coming up over the mountains, wrapped about with wisps of dusty pink cloud. We had sat in the old couple's parlour, talking of this and that. I must confess I can't resist these chats with the older citizens of the island. We will never see their like again. What is it they have which we have lost? 'The luxury of uneventful lives?'

Offering hospitality to my London guests, could I ever begin to match the dignity of Old Maria as, rising heavily from her chair, she moves purposefully in her dressing gown towards the parlour's refrigerator to offer me – horrors – a slice of cream cake. It is in three layers, has thick cream between each layer and glazed cherries on top. My dinner hour is approaching but never mind; acceptance is obligatory. Her parlour houses one armchair (hers), the said refrigerator, one dining chair (mine) and a spare bed (single) on which Old Kemon perches with his walking stick. He keeps his anorak on. The calor gas heater makes the tiny room stuffy but my feet begin to freeze through my shoes. The floor is of stone. Oh yes, there is a glass cabinet at the end of the bed in which are displayed an assortment of family photos and numerous bottles of Milk of Magnesia. The bed itself is permanently made up with clean sheets and pillowcase, ready for the visit of any of the three children, this year, next year perhaps? The 'girls' all live in the States. Kemon worked as a tailor in New York for thirty years. Maria refused to learn English. The girls married and settled but homesickness got the better of their parents and they returned. Rows of grandchildren, rarely seen, decorate the dresser.

Had he been to the coffee house today, I ask Kemon, or had the cold wind put him off?

'Of course I go! Every day I go and every evening. That is the way in Cyprus!'

Old Maria gives me a female look, full of meaning.

'And what about Maria?'

'Maria?' Kemon's face registers bewilderment. 'What has Maria to do with it? She must work in the house, of course! Now, she cannot make the lace. It is a pity.'

Kemon, whose namesake, he tells me, was one of Greece's most illustrious warriors, is exerting his authority.

Maria gives me another look, rueful and resigned. Without the lace-making she has lost the companionship of the other women. But, apart from that, she keeps her own counsel. She has lived abroad for many years and that has made a difference. Her companions are her prayer book and her radio.

'Perhaps the women should have a coffee shop?' I suggest.

'The women? They go to church. That is their coffee shop!'

Kemon chuckles at his little joke, then taking his stick asks if I would like to do a tour of the rest of his house. This takes less than three minutes.

'This is our restaurant!' Kemon waves his stick at the kitchen door. As there is room to hold only one person at a time, we peer through the door. Inside, the contents are ancient and very basic. We progress across the courtyard. Some lemon trees occupy most of it, a washing line strung between them. In the only bedroom two iron bedsteads repose on a stone floor as bare as a melon skin. The gas fire is off and the temperature within would be ideal for setting a jelly. From a cupboard, Kemon produces an electric pad he has brought back for Maria from the States. At some time during their retirement the daughters have treated their parents to a visit. Kemon tells me he can do without such fancy things as 'electric hot water bottles'.

'Soon, we will be in the best town,' he announces cheerfully, as we return to the tiny parlour. He points at the ceiling with his stick. 'It will be very good.'

Knowing how strenuously the old couple have resisted all efforts by their three daughters (one of whom visited recently) to move them into the home for the elderly in the upper village, Kemon's remark surprises me.

'You mean you will move into the home in Pano L—?'

'No. No.' Kemon waves his stick again with some impatience. 'I mean God's town! It is the best place. It will not be too hot and it will not be too cold. And the people, they will be nice. We must wait!' he adds with a chuckle.

FEBRUARY

Tuesday

Achilles has gone into the Army: Evagora's fears have been realized. She has been crying again. It would seem that the opportunities for bullying the underdog in army life are plentiful and that these young conscripts can have a hard time. With the knowledge that two of her sons have been through it already and that after Achilles, there is one more to go, Evagora's spirits have been very low.

This afternoon, I walked with two village women and Androulla up the long, high hill to the chapel of Ayios Georgiou. This little chapel is so sky-bound it would make a splendid perch for angels. The two sisters do the walk daily throughout the year in all weathers as well as tending to the other five chapels, which are a good deal more accessible. We were breathless from the climb. Once inside Ayios Georgiou, our presence made the tiny place seem crowded. The others set about their first duty of kissing the icons, of which about a dozen at least take up a great deal of the wall space. The icon of St George is prominent. Then they saw to the candle. This is got ready by filling a glass tumbler with water and then adding a dash of oil. (Cooking oil will do, Androulla explained.) On the surface a tiny wick is floated, held aloft by an equally tiny 'platform' of cardboard or cork. The wick will burn for twenty-four hours.

On a table in a corner were homely household items – cans of Coca Cola, lemonade and a bottle of sunflower oil. On the lectern rested four rolls of lavatory paper.

'Does the priest hold services here very often?' I asked in my pidgin Greek.

'Once a year, on St George's Day.'

On the telephone this evening, I recounted my visit to Maria. 'I owe St George a big thank-you,' she told me. 'Did I tell you how he found my painting for me?'

85

'No, go ahead.'

'It was like this. I was having an exhibition in Larnaca and a friend had helped me strap my biggest and best canvas on to the roof of my car. When we got to Larnaca we found that the canvas had gone. Blown away! So we had to turn round and drive all the way back, slowly, slowly, looking and looking, but we could see nothing. Then, you know, just as we were going up our last big hill, what do you think? There was my painting propped against his little mountain! I think St George must have been smiling on me. I sold that painting for a very good sum and I can tell you, Leez, I was needing the money very badly. Will you help me plant two trees up there?'

'Yes, if you do the digging.'

Thursday

We are nearing the end of February and the dams are dangerously low. From our roof terrace we can see our own dam down in the valley barely one third full. Neither the torrential rains nor the melting snows on Mount Olympus have filled them. They say that skiers on the Troodos have been few and that the snowfalls grow lighter with each passing winter.

There is talk in the papers that the Turks have offered us water, 'the water of peace' they call it. So far there has been no response from the Greek Cypriot government. *The Cyprus Weekly* suggests that an exchange be made: Turkish water for Greek Cypriot electricity.

'The Government's official policy on the continuing drought seems to coincide with that of the church – pray for rain', comments an exasperated leader writer. 'Turkey, however, not too reliant on the goodness of Allah, is planning to transport water through a pipeline from the mainland and to offer it to other countries in the region. To accept the offer requires the kind of vision that would also resolve the island's growing labour shortage by employing out of work Turkish Cypriots,' the writer continues. 'But of course it would be too much to expect of our government to consider taking water from Turkey, even though it makes perfect sense.'

Our valley, however, is now as green as the Emerald Isle, in parts. The almond trees are burgeoning with new buds about to dot the landscape with puffballs of palest pink, while at their feet are hints of the gentle asphodel. The delicate yellow of the charlock and brighter yellow of the buttercup are scattered over the sheltered dells and along the roadside verges. Only a tell-tale pallor near the roots of the spring crops and on the tips of the pines suggests that, once again, the rains are disappointing. Water, we are told, or rather the lack of it, will soon become one of the great political issues of the Eastern Mediterranean, greater than any squabbles over borders.

Friday

This weekend Greek Cyprus is voting for a new President but election fever has barely rippled the surface in our small village. Those who favour the steady leadership of the status quo support the ageing Mr Glafcos Clerides. Something tells us that Mr C has nothing to fear in our neck of the woods.

In the Turkish occupied north of the island Mr Rauf Denktash reigns supreme. Last summer Mr Clerides and Mr Denktash signed an agreement that would allow both sides of Cyprus to exchange information on the 'whereabouts of the graves of missing persons'. Like many other sensitive matters here, this question has been shelved since 1974, the year of Turkey's invasion of the north. About 1,600 Greek Cypriots are still unaccounted for, as are about 803 missing Cypriot Turks.

Mr Rauf Denktash and Mr Glafcos Clerides are both roly-poly men, the latter a far more politically reasonable character than the former. They were boyhood friends at school but now face each other across the UN Buffer Zone that cuts the city of Nicosia in half and divides the island. The Turks grabbed roughly one third of the north. Now that the Berlin Wall is down, Nicosia is the only capital city in the world that is still divided politically and militarily, with mutual distrust the cement that keeps the divide in place.

These two portly politicians, who hold so much power in their hands, are backed up by the two countries of Greece and Turkey; the latter is a good deal more powerful than the former and the northern section of our island is only forty miles from Turkey's shores. But it must be remembered that it was the four Greek Colonels attempting to overthrow the democratically elected government of Cyprus that spurred Turkey to invade.

When asked what he hoped to gain at one of the interminable rounds of 'talks' about The Cyprus Problem, Mr Denktash, noted for his wit as well as his appetite, replied 'a good afternoon tea'. Eating and manoeuvring are two of this man's chief delights, the other being taking photographs of the beauties of the Northern Cyprus landscape, which he has published in book form to rub more salt into the Greek Cypriot wound. Mr Denktash's policy is to alter the character of the north by flooding the region with over eighty thousand Anatolian peasants. Nothing is done for these peasants once they arrive and their lives remain ones of want and toil. Rauf Denktash has agreed, however, that the Turkish north occupies more than its fair share of the island and that if the territory was reduced (as proposed) by ten per cent, this would give around ninety thousand Greek Cypriot refugees a chance to return to their homes.

Monday

I have joined The American Archaeology Society and this evening Tim and I attended a lecture on Middle Eastern pottery. (I have already forgotten the exact period – Late Helladic, thirteenth

century BC, or did he say Early Canaanite?) Our lecturer spoke in muffled tones and his slides consisted mainly of graphs of eye-crossing dullness. Tim was soon asleep with his long legs stretching under the chairs of the people in front. My mind wandered badly. There were also some black and white slides of shards. The audience was told that after months of digging and research and using the latest scientific equipment, our lecturer was able to analyse his finds. His conclusions were that the particular pots, on which he is now an expert, had been made in the *same area* as the clay that had formed them. No one still awake in the audience seemed surprised by this startling announcement and a very short question time followed.

Next month there is to be a talk on Aphrodite, which, we expect, will be studded with references to fertility rites, sacrificial bulls and other heady stuff.

Wednesday

The English couple have invited us to drinks. Things are looking up.

Perhaps we will be friends?

MARCH

Sunday

Today, 2nd March, is the first day of the *Nestia* (Lent). The church bells began ringing at 4 p.m. The priest was wearing a robe of scarlet brocade embroidered with panels of gold. The gas heaters were alight although the afternoon was warm. I left my lighted candle with all the others and sat beside Old Anna so that she might help me to follow some of the proceedings. I noticed Kemon in one of the front pews, while Maria sat at the back, as usual, with the women.

On the short walk back to their house I took Maria's arm while Kemon struggled along on his stick. Swallows swooped overhead and a dog on its chain barked noisily.

'Oh be quiet you!' said Kemon. On we went up the hill.

'Our life is over' said Kemon. 'We do not have much more days left.'

'I might die before you, Kemon. We don't know how long we have.'

'I do not say you might die before me! I just say we don't have much days left!'

'Are you frightened?'

'No. I am not frightened because I have not many things I have done against. Some leetle sins, perhaps.' He smiled mischievously. 'We all sin. But I hope God forgives me. If he does not,' he pondered, his eyes twinkling, 'I will be all alone.'

We took our seats in the small parlour. I could sense the old couple's unease. The fast had begun and must last for fifty days. No animal products must be eaten and this eliminated cakes and biscuits and Maria's favourite little *courapiedies*.

'I won't stay,' I said. 'I must get home and cook dinner.'

Their relief was almost comical.

'*Kalinichta*, Leez. *Sto kalo*.'

91

Tuesday

Early March. Glorious morning. A pair of swallows sit preening their feathers on the telegraph wires. The feathers have a glossy midnight blue sheen. Second swallow makes an attempt to mate with first swallow. First swallow protests. 'Can't you see I've flown all the way from Africa?' she asks. 'Give me a moment to relax, please!'

Monday

Still not enough rain. On the plains around Nicosia the eucalyptus and pines are half dead with thirst. In the mountains things are better.

Having not seen Madonna for a week, I went down in the evening with half a loaf of stale bread. The yard gate was open, the water trough empty and there was no sign of her. I wandered about, stepping through the lush pasture which is now head high. Where the tops of the vegetation end, the pink almond blossom begins and above the blossom a pale pink evening sky. I came across a familiar 'crop circle' in the pasture where Madonna had eaten recently but apart from one or two clumps of manure, there was no sign of her.

'Madonna!'

Two disembodied brown ears, some twenty yards distant, appeared above the burgeoning puffs of fennel.

'Madonna, you funny old thing. I thought I'd lost you.'

Saturday

With spring around the corner the visitors are beginning to line up again! The first are Tim's parents.

Today, there was yet another long-distance call from Tim's

mother. She and Ralph will visit us next month. Diana is in search of further reassurance about our village hotel.

'Now, firstly, dear, are you quite sure about the beds? Two single beds, not a double?'

'Yes.'

'Good, I simply can't stand double beds. I haven't slept with Ralph for years and don't intend to start now.'

I recall a telephone conversation with Anna some weeks ago. We had discussed the arrival of Tim's mother in considerable detail. Anna had been adamant about the beds.

'Now, about a refrigerator,' Diana continued. 'Will there be one?'

'Anna will put the only refrigerator she has into your room.'

'Good. In that case I will bring plenty of cheese.'

'Oh, but there's no need to do that! Cyprus is positively stiff with cheeses.'

Diana ignored my advice and hurried on.

'About early morning tea. Will there—?'

'The hotel doesn't have the staff for early morning tea. But I will lend you our kettle and a teapot.'

'I don't eat breakfast' said Diana, ignoring my offer. 'I just have coffee. Ralph, on the other hand, likes one piece of toast and some marmalade. Is there a balcony in our room? You know I'm bringing a stick? It would be helpful if we had our own balcony. My hip is not too good.'

A little puzzled by the connection between these two, I said yes, yes, goodbye and hung up, thankful that Diana's phone bills are hers and not ours. This last call at midday and on a weekday had lasted a good fifteen minutes.

I drove up to the top village to see Anna and reassure myself again on the above-mentioned points. Forgetting the hour, I interrupted her mid-afternoon siesta.

'You don't have a twin-bedded room with a balcony, do you?' I enquired apologetically, noting Anna's bleary-eyed response to my call. 'Tim's mother has changed her mind.'

'I have one double room with a balcony, yes Leez, but it has the matrimonial bed.'

Anna's heavy pronunciation of the word 'matrimonial' conjured up tiresome moments of wifely duty rather than ethereal transports of conjugal bliss.

'I'm afraid that the matrimonial bed is out,' I told her, but refrained from going into further explanations, much as Anna might appreciate them.

'What else have you got? With a balcony?'

'There is your room. Yours and Teem's. You always liked that room.' She lit a cigarette. She is a heavy smoker.

'Um. Yes. That's true.'

I hedged a bit. We had liked the room because of its sunny aspect and the little balcony that hung over the street, so that we could watch the world go by. What we did not care for, however, were the noises from Mr Christis' Cypriot Delight factory next door. At nine o'clock sharp every morning strange *thump-thumping* noises emanated from its depths like the insistent beat of the tom tom. What could Mr Christis be doing to his Cypriot Delight?

Out of curiosity one day I had paid a visit. Two great cauldrons of the stuff boil away in the back room, supervised by one of the granddaughters, while the other granddaughter fills the boxes in the front of the shop. There are different subtle, mouth-watering flavours – apricot, rose water, almond. Some have nuts and some are plain. Mr Christis himself sits outside a good deal, reading a newspaper. So engrossed was he on one occasion that a cauldron of the mixture got burnt and the old man was heavily reprimanded by his son, the co-proprietor. Delicious as the product is, the production of it would not appeal to Tim's mother.

'Have you somewhere quiet?'

'Come and I show you what I have, Leez.'

We settled, finally, for a three-bedded family room at the back of the hotel which has, in addition, a spacious balcony. The fact that the balcony overlooks the car park is unfortunate, but the car park is very small. The room itself is large and the third bed is positioned in a far corner. That should please Diana.

I muse on what a good thing Tim's relatives aren't arriving in mid-summer, when the hotel's water problems could become acute. On one busy weekend last July it gave out entirely for some twenty-four hours. Staying at the hotel ourselves during our search for a house to rent we shared the dismay of a group of hygiene-conscious Germans who appeared at breakfast with disconsolate faces.

'The lavatory in our room. It does not vork! We haf no vater!'

No problem, Anna assured us all. She had already telephoned her Expert. He would, or had, settled everything. By the evening, the Expert had settled nothing. It was all the fault of the mukhtar, Anna told us in confidence. Why did the mayor not realize the importance of water for the tourist industry? Her hotel should receive priority. The following morning, with the situation little better, the Germans left for the coast, forgoing their breakfast.

Today I wrote to mother, keeping the enclosed copy for reference, as this diary-writing is a little erratic.

We've had a bit of excitement here. Last week a Russian lady booked into Anna's hotel. The day after her arrival, she borrowed a bicycle and went off. By nightfall, as she had failed to return, concern for her welfare began to mount. Anna telephoned Leonides, the local taxi driver and the Gay Lothario of the village. He wears a black leather jacket and a disrobing glance. Anna asked him would he please go in his taxi and look for the missing guest? There are many hairpin bends around here, few of them are clearly marked and the roads are steep.

Grumbling, Leonides set off in his taxi, a yellow Mercedes. He wore his usual sexy leather jacket, a trademark and a hit with the ladies. But the Russian lady is not beautiful. She encompasses her bulk in a shiny blue anorak and her muscles, she has many.

95

At 8.30 p.m. Leonides was back, Russian-less. As we sat sipping our drinks in the bar, we discussed the possible fate of Anna's latest guest. Anna's bicycle had no headlamp, the tyres were a bit dodgy and the weather was also dodgy. Suggestions for Stage Two were being bandied about when through the door of the vestibule strode our Russian, wheeling her bicycle, her face glowing a healthy pink beneath her white woolly hat. She beamed at us through a set of imperfect

teeth, rested her bicycle against the Reception desk and joined us.

She tells us her name is Nina. She is a doctor in Moscow, working with Aids sufferers. As soon as she gets home she will have her teeth removed. *Whoosh!* She makes a slicing movement with her hand. Just so. No problema! In Moscow the dentists are very good. The doctors are very good. Everything in Russia is very good. The hospitals, they are also very good. The Art! The paintings! We must all come to Russia to see them. But before that, her teeth must come out. She opens her mouth to demonstrate. We all agree the matter looks urgent.

There are more and more Russians here now, residents as well as tourists. They are not, as far as one can gather, popular. Rumours abound of money laundering, bouncing cheques etc.

All love

Libby

Wednesday

We have all of us got quite fond of good old Nina. Convinced that she must be lonely so far from home, we have had her over for coffee and I have escorted her down to Maria's studio to view 'some Cypriot art'. Back in the bar of the hotel for our sundowners, we all agree it is fun to have such a character in our midst, such a change to the ordinary run of tourist! Nina has an endless fund of anecdotes which, if linguistically a little hard to follow, are entertaining.

Anna comes by to join us for a few moments. As usual, she is tired.

'This man, he comes for a holiday from Sweden,' she tells us, lighting up yet another cigarette. 'Last night, at two o'clock, he telephones me. I am asleep, of course. He wants me to go to his room and put a bandage on his leg. It is hurting him, he says. I telephone the doctor. The doctor, he cannot come. I telephone the police. They cannot come. So I am the doctor!'

'What about the Mayor of—? Have you heard from him?'

'Yes,' Anna replies, giving us one of her rare smiles, which transforms her face. 'He comes next month. He telephones me every day. He wants I get him fresh prawns and flowers from Limassol and champagne. This morning he telephones me from Athens at five o'clock.'

The Mayor has booked the matrimonial suite (that rejected by Diana). We can all guess for whom it, the prawns and the champagne are intended. But can his wife?

'My friend from Ayia Napa,' Anna continues wearily, 'she telephones me at midnight. Her cat is dead. Last year it was her dog. I am tired. My neck is very stiff.'

Nina, who has entered at this moment with her bicycle, drops it and, springing at Anna, says, 'Come, come. I fix!'

Steering her patient on to an upright chair in the foyer, she begins a ferocious pummelling action on her spine.

'Ouch!' wails Anna.

'Good! Good!' says Nina, redoubling her efforts.

She begins a series of karate chops. Anna complains loudly but to no avail. Nina is determined to show us all that when it comes to remedial therapy, Russia once again leads the world. Then, without warning, she whips Anna's sweater from its anchorage and begins the pummelling action on bare flesh.

A bunch of new guests arrive, ready to check in. Their suitcases stand in the Reception area, their expressions are startled. But the patroness of the hotel and her therapist are too engrossed to notice them. As neither the guitar-strumming niece nor the would-be actress are anywhere to be seen, I go off to find Pavlos in the kitchen.

'Pull the blinds down,' I hiss at Maria as several faces in the street outside peer in. Half a remedy is better than none at all.

Pavlos appears, a good deal of flour on his apron and wearing a beaming smile. The new guests are mollified and follow him upstairs to their rooms.

Sunday

The second Sunday in Lent. The church this morning is packed. The six chandeliers sparkle with a myriad lights, the shimmering lamps enhance the gold of the icons. Several gas burners, together with lingering clouds of incense and the lit candles, add to the stuffiness. Some of the village men today are wearing suits. The mukhtar occupies a pew against a side wall, perhaps to keep us all in order. His small fair-haired grandson (with the Russian mother) balances beside him on the wooden arm of a pew and remains there, wrapt and attentive, for two full hours. He is swaddled in woollies against the imaginary cold.

At last when weariness is gripping one and all, it is the children's turn. Obediently they queue before the altar steps and wait patiently for some ten minutes until the priest appears from the door in the iconostasis. Each child receives his communion wine, Father S tilting the long handle of the ladling spoon over the recipient's nose so that every drop reaches its target. The grandson of the mukhtar smacks his lips. A toddler in her father's arms cries for more. The children scuttle back to their seats, munching their thick chunks of Lenten bread.

Monday

Tim has a new administrator called Katerina. She has sacked Tim's part-time secretary, which has been a shock. Tim has said little about her except to describe her as butch. As such women terrify him, we hope it does not bode ill. I noticed him helping himself to a third whisky this evening but he was reluctant to talk further

99

– how I wish men were good communicators! There seems to be something inbuilt in their psyche (and it can't be just an English upbringing) that acts like a blocked valve when a heart to heart threatens. For a start, communication, especially in English public schools, should be taught as a school subject.

Tuesday

On Cyprus television last night there was an unexpected announcement.

A Russian woman has been arrested in Nicosia. It seemed that her crime has been hopping to and fro across the border between the two communities, photographing 'sensitive' areas for the Turkish government. After a few more details, the newscaster pauses in order to allow the camera to home in. There – can it be true? Yes, as large as life is our Nina! Her white woolly hat is missing, to reveal a head of remarkably black hair. There is the shiny blue anorak all right, but the toothy grin has gone. Did they say six months? She appears to be wearing handcuffs and is in close proximity to a burly policeman.

'Are there army installations near us?' I asked Anna. Although I am still reeling from these revelations, Anna, as usual, was sanguine.

'But of course,' she shrugged. 'Nina, she is a spy. For the Turks, yes.'

'*No problema?*' I suggested.

Anna grinned. '*No problema,*' she agreed.

I have noticed on my trips down the mountain road a settlement that does not look like a settlement. Rather it is a collection of square buildings, all much the same. At night its lights twinkle mysteriously. Nina had not had far to go, even on a bicycle.

Friday

Our doorbell rings. Tim answers it. Evagora is there, pressing upon us three magenta-coloured eggs, hard boiled. All part of local Easter tradition, she explains. They have been boiled with the root of the lisari plant to achieve their striking colour, but they do not look appetizing. Is this lisari plant the henna which, in ancient times, was famous for its oils and salves? I must investigate.

Later there is another tap on the door, a rapping sound rather than a tap. It is Old Kemon with his stick.

'I am asking that the laundry man he comes to your house on Wednesday? You want him to come?'

'Yes, please Kemon. That would be most helpful.'

The laundry man calls once a week at the top end of the village. However, he is too far away for me to hear his van honking. From his seat under the mulberry tree, Kemon has overheard me telling the mukhtar's wife, Chrisso, that I can never send my dry cleaning because I can never catch the van. Normally, I doubt whether Kemon would have stirred himself as his hip is bad and he is slow and frail. However, since one of his daughters telephoned me from New York to pass on the message to her parents that she is coming 'home' in August, the old man has gained a new lease of life, in spite of his rigid Lenten diet. There is a fresh twinkle in his eye, a new spring in his step.

Saturday

O, the sheer joy of waking up to these early summer mornings! First light on the bougainvillaea outside our bedroom and the swallows swooping and weaving in and out under the eaves. Then early morning cuppas on the roof as we watch the great ball of the sun emerge from the sea, leaving behind its shimmering golden tails, the sea itself mysterious and brooding. The sheer joy of getting dressed into scanty clothing, all done in a minute!

This day so radiantly fair
Shall never into twilight pass.
The very surface of the air
Shines polished, like a looking glass.

Loud chatterings from the parrots and the rasping twitters from the baby swallows in their nest endorse our view that it is good to be alive.

Monday

Looking at old photographs of our home when we moved in, we are more than pleased with the changes we have made.

The ugly little settee in the front parlour is all but obliterated by a colourful Indian cover, the iron legs barely visible. Its hardness is softened by Thekla's old bed pillows under the cover. The plastic curtains here went very early on. Persian 'tablecloths' now disguise the mock-brass curtain rails. A giant looking glass with an elaborately carved wooden frame (Middle European?), given to Tim and somewhat outsized for this little room, adds a touch of distinction. A small painting of St Catherine of Sienna coexists happily with our Greek icons. The Pope (and I) sit on the bookshelf by the wood-burning stove. A rush mat warms the tiled floor in winter.

Tim has painted the parlour, the kitchen and the bathroom ivory white. Our sitting/dining room is long and low-ceilinged. Cool in summer, its eighteen inch thick walls provide useful window ledges for Roz's dried flowers and for our ornaments. Our Indonesian bookcase glows warmly in its rich red browns. Our antique dining chairs at the end cohabit well with Thekla's orange armchairs. They and the kitchen table are disguised with a batik tablecloth and numerous Indian throw-overs. A coffee table from the Thrift Shop winks in harmony with the bookcase. Some Persian rugs colour the grey tiled floor; our paintings bring cheer to the whole house.

Out in the courtyard and up on the roof terrace stand our sixty ceramic pots, splashes of colour from Lambros's garden centre. The Australian gravillea so beloved of the rainbow lorikeets back home, who look for its pink-blossomed honey, is paired off with a young mauve bougainvillaea. Our Norfolk Island pine, equally far from home, has grown a foot at least. Climbing ferns disguise the wire mesh of the aviary, their tendrils making appetizing treats for the parrots. A pink camellia echoes the many pinks of the hardy geraniums which will flower all year, if allowed. Wild mint, picked on a mountain walk, flourishes in a courtyard bed, as does the wild thyme.

We have erected screens of green mesh webbing as a sun shield on the roof. The grapevine itself makes a splendid giant umbrella, and the green mesh takes over where the vine leaves stop. Three white reclining chairs up here give the users' behinds a rest from Thekla's 'waffle-bottom' green ones. All in all, ours is a small paradise. Pleasures are transitory. Will ours last?

I have forgotten to mention the purchase of our African lovebirds, miniature parrots with pretty colourings of peach, green or blue. The first pair settled in so well we are tempted to get more. We have christened them Pinky and Perky. Some weeks ago we attached a nest box to the side of their cage and it was amusing to see the electrifying effect it had on Pinky. She cocked her head, peered closer, hopped over and examined the entrance hole with intense interest. A moment later she was inside! We have high hopes for the future and will build a proper aviary soon. At present it needs extending and given a more waterproof roof. It nestles against the west wall of the courtyard, an ideal spot.

Wednesday

Alas, I have missed the most important event in the church year, the Greek Orthodox Easter. A severe bout of flu, caught from Tim, has laid me low for a week. Not even here, breathing the fresh air of the mountains, do we escape the sinister bugs that seem to find most parts of the world nowadays.

Unaware of how infectious I was becoming, I went to five o'clock church last Wednesday and was thankful to see yesterday, as she passed our door, the elderly lady who had sat with me in our conjoined wooden pews. During the long days that followed I listened to the bells from my sick bed, rousing myself to watch the Easter Epitaphios Procession pass beneath the window, under the sparkling stars. It was heralded by the chattering of village folk and the laughter of children as they followed the flowers decked bier carrying the coffin through the lanes, the priest in front with his assistants. By the time the last house was blessed, Father S was all but tottering with exhaustion, so hot has the weather become, so heavy are his garments and so lengthy and numerous are the services. The procession stopped outside Old Crystalla's house, where I could see the old lady and Maroulla receive the blessing of Holy water and lay their gifts of rosewater and dried olive leaves on the bier.

On Good Friday, some of the village women remained in the church all night. Here all the icons were draped in black cloth. At midnight on Easter Saturday, the moment the children and young men had been waiting for arrived. The gigantic pile of dead branches and pieces of timber that had been building up all week was set alight – this to symbolize Christ's ascent into heaven. The bonfire was placed perilously close to a magnificent kermes oak beside the church. Indeed, a second oak was so badly scorched some years back that it never recovered and had to be chopped down. The bonfire was lit during the course of the service and as the flames rose higher and higher, the delighted shrieks of the children and the fizzing of fireworks competed with the voices of the indefatigable Father S and his chanters indoors. All this was related to me in detail by Tim, though I could hear well enough from my window the voices of revelry, mixed with those of devotion.

When all was quiet again, I peered out. A light in Old Crystalla's garden lit up the oddments on her washing line: Demetri's flannel shirt, a petticoat, some kitchen cloths. The stars glimmered palely as a light mist stole about and the echoes of the pealing bells continued their ghost-like progression across the listening mountains and down the valley to the quiet sea.

Thursday

A great deal of activity is going on in the aviary. Pinky has been in the nest box for weeks and now the pair of them are as busy as can be. We don't like to disturb the little family, so will await developments. Tim and I are due to fly to the UK next week for a brief visit, so Evagora will take on the responsibilities of birds and plants.

APRIL

Dearest Ma,

I'm very glad to hear the tree surgeon has only charged you half price for his clumsy work, though three hundred dollars still sounds a lot under the circumstances. Did he refund you for the deodar?

April has brought us some glorious spring weather just as you are going into autumn. I do so miss our Australian birds and feel so thankful Tim and I were able to 'catch up on them' during our time in Sydney, before coming here. When I tell people we had wild lorikeets in our harbourside garden they look at you in wonder. The Cypriot kills so many wild birds here. Consequently it is a thrill to have swallows nesting in our courtyard and this week the babies left the nest. What a chattering and a chittering is going on, not to be compared to our currawongs and magpies, but cheering to the spirits nonetheless. The parents spent the last week urging them on but the babies were determined not to budge. Our five fat fledglings seemed remarkably content with the cramped quarters of their tiny mud 'teacup' and would take it in turns to stack themselves in layers, two on top and three on the bottom and vice versa. A wing would stretch, a head that seemed all yellow beak and beady eye would peer over the edge and a fledgling would teeter on the rim, chattering hysterically and swaying like a drunk. 'Come on! Come on!' shrieked their parents, watching from the nearby bougainvillaea. Tim put a safety net below the nest, attached to the rafters. The courtyard floor is concrete hard.

Now the nest, alas, is empty but this evening the whole family was back, performing a joyful circuit of the courtyard, dodging the verandah railings and the clothes line with expert precision. They settled, all seven of them, on the clothes line at last, like a row of shiny, blue-black pegs. So unafraid are they that we can reach out and almost touch them. Tonight they roosted, some in the bougainvillaea and some under the eaves, close to their old home. Their arrival back caused great excitement in the aviary down below. Our African lovebirds, Pinky and Perky, have, also in our absence, hatched out four young. Lifting up the lid of their nest box, while Tim distracted them with their favourite meal of bougainvillaea blossoms, I spied the four babies, pink and nearly bald, little miniature Martians from outer space.

At ten o'clock, when the half moon was up, the nightingales started. We have not heard them before but the night seemed full of voices – over to the hill on the right, to the hills on the left and down below us, they kept up their unceasing song. They are on their migration and won't be here for long. As though not wishing to be outdone, our little scops owl flew at the naked bulb of our street light and then settled himself in one of the lloulloudia trees opposite, to begin his thin *ping ping* call to his mate. The light that dazzled our little owl now lights up a smart new street sign. Our donkey lane has now become Christaki Stefanou Avenue!

All love

L

Monday

A lovely week at Pissouri with Phoebe, Neil and the children. We rented two giant-sized apartments a couple of stones' throw from the sea but only Neil and Ewen braved the water. The rest of the time we used an outdoor pool where the water was somewhat less chilly. Being English, the family was satisfied with what it got. Our apartment building was surrounded by vineyards where the vines were sending forth their first leaves like pale green and pink tufts of crepe paper.

One day we took them home to the hills, where Agamemnon had a surprise ready. Madonna stood saddled in her yard, wearing her usual expression of stoic resignation.

'You will have a ride, I think?' Agamemnon beamed.

The invitation fell flat. Aware that our neighbour's son had gone to some considerable trouble on this, his precious Sunday off, I sprang into the saddle with somewhat less agility than they who 'brought the good news from Ghent to Aix'. Ewen then agreed to join me on the rock-hard little saddle, whereupon Hermione, aged four, and Helena, aged two, set up a series of loud shrieks. Whatever was Granny Libby *doing*?

Madonna behaved impeccably throughout and allowed the girls to offer her some tasty morsels of parsley hay and one or two pats on the nose. The weather turned unseasonally hot and, released from her duties in less time than she had dared to hope, she trotted happily back to her meadow, while Agamemnon joined us back home to partake of some iced lime juice.

Thursday

Melanie-of-the-carrots is not coming back. It transpires that her need for extra domestic work was accelerated by her son's forthcoming wedding. She has shown me photographs of her son, digging them out from the depths of her dilly bag, her face aglow with pride and perspiration in equal measure. He is a most handsome young man well worthy of his mother's adoration. I shall miss her, not for her slap-happy approach to her work but for her entertaining commentaries on people and life in general. Like many islanders, she has an insatiable curiosity for what-is-going-on and an equal enthusiasm for passing this on. Already several villagers have asked me if I am related to the Pope, my appearance in a black mantilla before the great man having convinced Melanie that His Holiness and I attended some family funeral service together. Other photographs of Tim in his barrister's wig have led her to a strong suspicion that he is a gentleman of sobering eminence.

Her son's wedding now out of the way (Tim and I were invited but had a previous engagement), Melanie has another reason for wishing to give up domestic work. She has the unmentionable piles (Evagora obliged here with some interpreting when Melanie grew desperate in her efforts to impart this information over a cup of coffee). However, her doctor is optimistic, and has given her some 'depositories' to cure the ailment.

We had a final coffee in the kitchen and shared a carrot and a bunch of grapes. I drove her to the lace shop in the upper village where she gains most of her employment, sitting on her wicker chair by the roadside and waving to passers by as she stitches (though how she will manage the sitting in her present condition is not clear). Some of the shop people up there are beginning to annoy the visitors with their constant soliciting and I fear Melanie is no different.

Sunday

Tim's parents have arrived. We met them at the airport, his mother in a wheelchair.

'We were two and a half kilos overweight,' was Diana's opening remark. 'If Ralph had brought less luggage we would have been all right.'

As Tim loaded their stuff into the boot of our Mazda (it being thought more politic to bring it rather than subjecting the old couple to the Rover's worn springs) we noted that Ralph possessed a case so small it resembled little more than an overnight bag.

We drove homewards, Diana commenting on her bad legs, her general exhaustion from the flight and her concern over the possible inadequacies of the village hotel.

'I *had* thought that Ralph would go before me,' she sighed

heavily. 'Thought so for years. However, now it looks as if *I* might go first.'

Silence greeted this remark until a quiet voice from the back seat was heard to mutter, 'Well, I'm doing my best.'

In the village hotel there were teething problems to overcome, as Diana had foretold.

Tim is straightway dispatched to buy stronger light bulbs and a correctly fitting bathplug. 'We are not in India, I hope?' There is an irritating luminous bedside clock whose flashing light will keep Diana awake. The beds are very narrow (but then, has not the matrimonial bed been scorned?) At any rate, Diana's bed must be moved from here to there. No handrails by the bathtub means that poor Ralph is stranded like a beached whale! Diana feels it safer to forgo a bath altogether, and as there is no shower she makes do with a soap and flannel sluicing at the wash basin. It is unfortunate that the funny little man at his Cypriot Delight shop chooses to open up *quite* so early (sounds do carry in a village, don't they?) and, these Greeks from Athens, they eat so terribly late, out by the pool and make such a noise about it! Could someone ask the nice girl in the dining room (Droulla, is it? Or Soulla? I can never remember) to make a really *hot* cup of coffee? Ralph does so like his coffee to be hot – and what extraordinary toast! All criss-crossed like a hot cross bun and quite soggy in the middle. Cheese at breakfast! Well, it does bring back memories of our posting in Finland. Ralph's egg was a little overdone this morning – rock hard, in fact – but there we are! Perhaps Droulla or Soulla can organize a more satisfactory egg tomorrow?

All these early hiccups are cancelled out, however, by the success of the fifty-fifth wedding anniversary lunch that Tim had arranged for his parents at Happy Valley. Pauline and Achilleas have turned themselves inside out for the occasion. The fare is part way between traditional Cypriot and haute cuisine. Some of our guests are Cypriot, including the mukhtar and his wife and Nicos and Panyiotis from the garage (the latter arrives looking as handsome

113

as Tom Cruise and bearing a pot of pink cyclamen tied up with many ribbons). There is also the elderly Dr D, one of the few Turkish Cypriots left in these parts, a distinguished and much respected figure. Some English friends and Maria represent the top village, and the gathering in all amounts to some forty people. Anna, as usual, is too busy at the hotel to come.

Guests arriving for the celebration are greeted outside the restaurant with Achilleas' hand-painted sign HAPPY VALLEY. WHERE PEOPLE SAY I GLAD I STOP. Indoors, Pauline's mother-in-law's handmade tablecloths are cleanly washed and protected with transparent plastic sheeting. Pauline, who hails from Yorkshire, knows well with what relish the Cypriot tackles his food. Achilleas has done the table decorations himself – sprigs of wild flowers in glass ashtrays. In season his orchard next door groans with fruit which guests can pick themselves, and if they wish leave a donation on the verandah table. In spite of the warm weather, Achilleas sports an English tweed cap, also a white apron, and waits on table. Two of his friends help out behind the bar.

Diana, who has announced several times that she intends to make a speech, does so. Twice this week she has had her hair 'done' – washed and blue rinsed – trusting herself to the village beauty salon. Her nails are manicured and wondrously scarlet, and come into much play as she emphasizes her points. She talks for a good half-hour, giving us a résumé of her life as a diplomatic wife in faraway places. One or two of her stories are decidedly risqué and I am thankful that the mukhtar and his wife, particularly his wife, aren't understanding a word. One of Diana's more respectable anecdotes is about their forced exodus from the British Embassy in Cairo during the six-day war with Israel. It surprises none of us present to hear that she herself had taken charge of operations. When a member of staff suffered a fatal heart attack during the hasty evacuation, Diana directed that the poor fellow be put in the Embassy swimming pool. Presumably, there was no water in it? She didn't say.

By the time Ralph's turn for speech-making comes around there seems little left for him to add. He puts down the success of their marriage to the fact that he is 'a good listener'.

Tuesday

Friends have offered to drive Diana down to Limassol to shop and Ralph has been ordered to attend, so today I am minding Maria's gift shop. We have just re-attached The Gallery Shop sign to the street lamp outside. A passing truck knocked it sideways last week. Maria stood on a chair by the doorstep attempting to thread a piece of wire through a pin-sized hole well above her head. I held the chair steady.

'Try not to make me laugh. This is hard enough to do as it is. And why are you clutching my shirt?'

'Moral support,' I tell her.

We are praying for some customers so I have agreed to shop sit for today, just in case. Maria has gone off to do her chores, feed her eleven cats (or is it fifteen?) and see to a box of silkworms someone has given her.

An hour goes by and a smartly dressed Italian with her husband enters. Her handbag is Gucci. '*Bon giorno.*' This is more or less the limit of my Italian.

The wife wants to know the price of a pottery dish which is marked at nine pounds. No, too much. She offers seven pounds. I glance over the road at Zanthe, who is sitting outside her sweet shop. Using sign language we agree that eight pounds is fair. 'Seven pounds – *Sette*,' insists the husband. I won't budge so they move off. Their expressions are not friendly.

Meanwhile an elderly resident on a donkey passes. He has two enormous bundles of hay strapped to his wooden saddle and he wears a rag hat. The donkey's hooves make a gentle *tap-tapping* on the stones.

More Italians come in, obviously on a bus tour. A determined-looking female takes a fancy to a painted pottery egg.

115

'*Quanto?*'

I can't find the price under the egg. She roots around and finds an egg with the price on it – four pounds. She likes it and hands me a ten pound note. Maria's petty cash tin has five pounds only. I run across the lane to Zanthe, who, although busy with another group of tourists, obligingly changes the ten-pound note.

'How much is the little bell?' demands my customer, but there's no price on that either.

'Free? *Libre?*' she asks, unsmiling.

Before I have time to decide on a price she has gone.

More women and a man come in. We are having quite a day. They inspect the T shirts. We measure up one of the women against one of the shirts, a navy one with a striking design of ancient-Greek motifs. But the shirt is pronounced too small. She is, she says, too fat. We inspect an identical shirt which I get on to a chair to unhook from the wall. This is for her son, who isn't present. But she thinks it won't fit. He is too tall. We shrug at each other in agreement that life is indeed difficult, and the party exits.

A gentle young woman asks about a small clay lamp. I explain to her it is a copy of an ancient Roman oil lamp. I try also to explain that it is ornamental only and that when Tim and I tried to use ours it burst into flames. She seemed to get the idea but bought it.

Total takings for the morning – ten pounds.

This afternoon was growing a little tedious until a French mother and daughter enter. The daughter takes a fancy to a bunch of dried pomegranates hanging on a peg.

'*A vendre?*' the daughter asks.

They are, in fact, a part of Maria's décor, but times are hard. I nod and then call across to Zanthe. It transpires that the pomegranates are actually hers and that she has lent them to Maria. However, she is willing to sell them. She suggests two pounds and whispers to me that Maria must keep the money. We agree she needs encouragement when entering the cut-throat world of commerce for the first time. With satisfied *au revoirs*, mother and daughter leave.

As I pop the twelve pounds takings into the drawer with the petty cash tin I see a note in Maria's hand-writing: *Liz, try to discourage the shop women sitting right outside my door!*

I will have to tell her that a percentage of the day's takings have come about through the generosity and presence of mind of one of them.

Wednesday

The shopping expedition went well yesterday and Diana appeared refreshed by the experience, if not Ralph. Noticing the good quality of leather goods made on the island, she had decided then and there to kit out her four grandsons with leather belts. However, as the boys are of varying ages and sizes, this led to a certain amount of complication. A daughter in Hampshire had to be telephoned from Limassol and enquiries made as to the waist measurements of the boys. As two of these were not hers, but belonged to her sister, a return call followed, involving a considerable wait. At the same time Diana had decided to kit out all six grandchildren with trainers, which are very cheap here as well as being well made. Shoe sizes therefore had to be calculated, and more phone calls ensued.

We are hoping that the friends who were kind enough to offer Tim's parents a lift to town will not bear us any malice.

MAY

Monday

Our *Cyprus Weekly* reports that the United States and the European Union do not think that the deployment of Russian anti-aircraft missiles in our part of Cyprus is a good idea. It will 'provoke Turkey'. Our Minister of Defence retorted that the missiles will be cancelled only if Cyprus is reunified or demilitarized. 'We cannot accept selective sensitivity,' he said. 'The Turks are strengthening their position in the Occupied North with tanks and mobile artillery.'

It is not often that Tim and I hear a Greek Cypriot politician willing to admit that Greece shares a good deal of the blame for this Turkish aggression. After the Second World War, with Britain still in charge in Cyprus, the young Bishop Makarios organized a plebiscite which produced a 96 per cent majority in favour of *Enosis* (union with Greece). Greece, seeing that Britain had no intention of losing Cyprus, sided with Cyprus while Turkey claimed the island to be part of the Turkish mainland. And so it went on. From 1955–59 the Greek Cypriots mounted a liberation struggle against British rule and in 1960 Cyprus gained its independence with Britain, Greece and Turkey standing as guarantors. Britain, however, was allowed to keep two sovereign bases. Makarios became President of the new Republic and a chap by the name of Fazil Kucuk was elected unanimously as Vice President by the Turkish Cypriots. The new President soon proposed a number of amendments to the Constitution 'to make it more workable' but Turkey objected. Fighting broke out all over the island. In the summer of 1963 over five hundred people were killed, the Turkish airforce attacked Greek Cypriot positions, the Turkish Cypriots fled into ghettos and Makarios began to be looked upon abroad as a 'kind of Castro in priest's clothing'. However, as the economy improved for the Greek Cypriots, they began to lose interest in

Enosis and to settle down to making money. Tourists were discovering the island's beauties. The Greek Government, run by four bullying colonels, did not like this change of tack, did not like Makarios and decided to get rid of him. On 15 July 1974 Nicosia was suddenly rocked by gunfire and the Presidential Palace went up in flames. Makarios himself fled and, swallowing his pride, took shelter in the British base of Akrotiri. A right-wing radical named Nikos Sampson, a mass murderer of Turkish Cypriots in the 1963–64 civil war, became President, with the Greek colonels' blessing.

Here Greece made a big mistake. Turkey, having threatened to act if its Muslim brothers were threatened, did so. This happened at daybreak five days later, on 20 July. The fiasco brought down the Greek Junta in Greece two days later. A moderate Cypriot, Glavkos Clerides, became President in Nicosia and democracy was back. However, Turkey wasn't taking chances. Greek Cypriots in their thousands fled before the advancing Turks, who finally took possession of 37 per cent of the island. These Greek Cypriots lived in refugee settlements, some of them for thirty years, never to return to their homes, while some thirty thousand Turkish Cypriots fled north. Hundreds of Greek and Turkish Cypriots were taken prisoner, never to be seen again. Nearly every family on the island lost a member in the fighting, around six thousand people all told, in the summer of 1974.

Here now in the south, at the end of the twentieth century, prosperity reigns. Only the ugly tenement blocks outside Nicosia, built for the refugees in the seventies, remind us of those desperate times. Living in such conditions was anathema to rural Greek Cypriots, many of whom built themselves new houses, got jobs in tourism and the manufacturing industries and, in record time, pulled themselves up by their boot straps. Not so in the north, where many go on living in rural poverty.

JUNE

Wednesday

Through my afternoon siesta comes the staccato chattering of our African parrots, louder than usual. I take no notice and eventually peace and quiet settles. Sipping iced tea about four o'clock, for the days are mighty hot, I let my gaze wander towards the aviary. Pinky is on her favourite perch but she is not returning to her nest. This is her second brood. A great stillness hangs over the afternoon. Slowly I become aware that things are not as they ought to be. Something is missing. There is no sign of Perky. Is he in the nest box? He is a good parent and shares the responsibility for feeding his young, which involves a rather unpleasant job of regurgitating his food. This he does with Pinky perched beside him, tilting her head sideways and keeping up a persistent tapping on his beak until he delivers the goods. It all looks rather painful but Perky presses on, manfully.

Now there is no sign of him. My eyes wander to the aviary door. The top half is open by several inches. I have forgotten to close the latch! As though reading my thoughts, Pinky cocks her head at me, a look of accusation in her beady eye.

I tell Evagora and Myrafora, who are out in the lane, stitching. They are very sorry. We all start calling. Pinky joins in with a positive racket of screeches and chattering, dashing from one end of the aviary to the other. Once or twice she makes as if to enter the nest box but, torn between wifely and motherly duty, darts off again.

'Leez! Leez! I can see the parrot!' Evagora's ten-year-old son, Michaelis, rushes in. 'In the tree! In the tree!'

Sure enough, perched on a high branch of the loulloudia across the lane, is Perky. But he is Perky no longer. A rather frightened little blue parrot is wondering what his world has come to. I call and call but it is Pinky's distracted cries that encourage her husband

120

homewards. Together we entice him on to the roof terrace, then on to the verandah railings and finally onto the roof of the aviary. Through the wire netting husband and wife attempt an ecstatic reunion but the two lovers who kiss and coo cannot quite meet. Pyramus and Thisbe have nothing on these two. Pinky's joy is touching. We have Perky almost in, when a thudding and bellowing of boys in the lane as they kick a football about scares our hero off again. Up, up he soars and far away!

'We'll have to let Pinky out too,' says Tim, on his return from the office. 'They'll be better off together.'

'But what about the babies?'

'I'll take them to Anthony tomorrow. I have to go to Nicosia anyway. I'll go to the pet shop first thing.'

From the giant palm tree in Crystalla's and Demetri's garden we can hear muted chattering as the two adult birds settle down for their first night of freedom. Meanwhile, in the nest box, we hope that the fledglings will survive the night. We have covered them with cotton wool.

Thursday

An early telephone call this morning from Tim in Nicosia. The baby parrots have been given vitamin supplements by kind Anthony, who rushed to the chemist next door to purchase these, plus an eye dropper.

'Each birt, he must have somesing to eat. You must do it like theese.' Anthony demonstrated the feeding procedure with the use of the eye dropper.

'How often do I have to do that?' Tim asked, aghast.

'Every hour you must to feed.'

'Every hour?'

'Yes. Otherwise they die.'

'Well,' Tim replied. 'They survived the night.'

Halfway down the motorway from Nicosia Tim stopped the

Rover on the hard shoulder to feed his ravenous family. He arrived back at 10 a.m., the nest box of babies under one arm and two brand new parrots in a cage under the other.

'I have a surprise for you,' I told him before he could deliver his. 'Pinky and Perky are back. I think they missed the children. Besides, they are ravenous.'

'Well, now we've got an extended family. What shall we call these two?'

'Let's call them Pyramus and Thisbe. Do you think they'll be as much in love as the others?'

Monday

Nellie, who 'does' for us, did not turn up this morning. She comes at seven, before the heat of the day builds up. By nine o'clock the village women have got the bulk of their housework done – the sweeping of the lanes, the watering of plants, the washing hung out, the beds made. However, a sustaining meal at midday and again in the evening is de rigueur and the ladies go about their duties with a kind of plodding fortitude. In the afternoons it is time to put out the low rush chairs and stitch the linen. Now and then a light breeze might blow, but on most days the heat lies like a great blanket and only the trilling of the cicadas breaks the stillness of the air. The women, however, talk. Their incessant day-long chatter is a source of wonder to the outsider. Seeing each other as they do, day long and every day, for mostly they never leave the village from one year to the next, what do they talk about? At seven in the morning they meet at the top of the village for the arrival of the truck from the small grocery shop in the top village. Throughout the day they meet again – for the arrival of the baker's van, the laundry van, the portable clothes shop, a rival greengrocer, the butcher. Always there is talk. There is no loneliness here. The spectre of being shut away and forgotten in old age is unknown. On every family outing granny, always in black, makes up the numbers. Sometimes there is grandfather. Families meet up every Sunday, unfailingly. In the towns it may be different but this tradition, though now perhaps resented by the young, holds. As a Western grandmother, I am a little envious.

At nine o'clock I went round to see if Nellie was unwell. New sewerage pipes are being laid in her lane and I picked my way over mounds of rubble to her door.

'Who are you looking for, Liz?' bellows a voice.

It is Nicos, supervising two workmen who are laying cables alongside the pipes. Nicos fancies himself as an electrician.

'Nellie,' I tell him.

'She's still asleep. She's not well.'

He nods in the direction of one of the workmen, who confirms this. I hear a noise in Nellie's kitchen, so I cross her courtyard. Nellie is standing by her sink, a forlorn figure. She explains in halting English that she has a headache and has forgotten everything. She points to a case of tinned foodstuffs on the floor and then at a bedroom above the courtyard. It is empty. Her only daughter has gone to Moscow!

'To Moscow?'

'*Ne. Ne.* To Moscow. She must study there for five years.'

No. No. She cannot come home! It is too far. Moscow is cheaper than England, but Nellie must send her food, nonetheless. Nellie has cried for three days.

I commiserate as best I can. For once, language difficulties do not get in the way. We agree that being a mother is very hard.

'She says she'll come to you this afternoon,' bellows Nicos through the front door.

'Is she sure? It will be *poli zesty* by then.'

'Look, Liz, do you want her to clean your house or don't you? Christ! I dunno!'

All right, all right, I agree. Nellie can come, though the heat of afternoon will make us both wish that she hadn't.

Wednesday

Achilles the beautiful is looking for a temporary job. Evagora is so happy to have him home. He has six months' respite before he must return to the Army. As far as his mother is concerned it is a death knell. Evagora's sweet face creases with anxiety. Achilles is better now, yes, but he is not yet fully recovered. The mental scars of his ordeal remain. Some of the boys are bullied, some are not. She does not know why but what can they, as a family, do?

'Did you report the bullying?'

'Oh yes. Of course! We reported it but they do nothing. The Army is like that. It is famous for it. My other boys, they didn't get bullied. But Achilles, yes.'

Achilles comes out of the house as we talk. He is carrying a bucket of slops for his father's dogs down on the farm. He plonks it into the back of the old utility truck that takes up most of the space in the lane. His army haircut has played a certain havoc with his good looks. In his jungle greens and with a shaved head it is difficult to spot our Rudolph Valentino. He allows me a sheepish smile.

Friday

The dull thudding of machinery denotes that the workmen are still labouring on the new chapel down below the village. It will be dedicated to St Raphael. From our breakfast table on the roof terrace we can make out the tall dark figure of Father S putting his shoulders to the wheel with the best of them. His long garments must hamper his efforts, to say nothing of the discomfort as the midsummer sun gathers strength.

An old man walks carefully downhill towards the chapel. The ground drops away steeply and he picks his way slowly. The dry grass is as tall as he is and the dead heads of the fennel even taller, but this does not deter him from lighting a cigarette. He prods about with his walking stick. Once his cigarette is finished he produces a blue plastic bag from his pocket and from a low green bush he begins plucking something. Berries? I must ask Evagora what it is he is picking. One can feel the heat of the sun on his back as he stoops. Yet it is only eight in the morning.

This afternoon, on the low road that leads past the new chapel, I spied the spritely figure of Old Demetri cantering home on Madonna, his saddle bags bulging from a shopping spree in Pano L—. His back is straight as an arrow. Years of practice have hardened his posterior to such an extent that he seems indifferent to the fact that the saddle is made of wood and sacking and that Madonna's gait must be about as comfortable as a car without springs.

A number of the village people use this little road to get to their plots of land in the valley and rumour has it that they are now having a battle with the Greek Orthodox Church, which, for some perverse reason, wishes to close the road off at the chapel.

JULY

Sunday

'Aren't you coming to the festival?' asked a cheerful face at the steering wheel, as I edged past his truck in the lane. 'The festival for the new church!'

'What time does it start?'

'Now. Six thirty.'

A truckload of faces beamed from the interior. I recognized Panicos and his wife among them.

'Thank you. We didn't know.'

I collected Tim and we set off down the dirt road past the cemetery, around tortuous bends, up hill and down dale. Tim's heavy old Rover was like a wheezy dinosaur. Nicos, who had often told us how beautiful it was down by the dam, arrived there with his old mother at the same time as us, and he and Tim helped the old lady up the last steep incline to the little white church at the top. Newly planted shrubs – oleander and lantana – and geraniums and small poplar trees and grapevines bordered the path, somehow all taking root in the bone-dry soil. The new church, a charming little building of sparkling white with a wooden bell tower, for reasons of cost as well as manpower perhaps, is not built of the usual local stone. It is perched on a spur that overhangs the steep descent to the dam, which is now pitifully low in water. Not just a poor winter's rainfall but the burning sun has all but sucked it dry. Perhaps at the inauguration service prayers will be said for rain.

Some sensible folk had brought folding chairs, for the tiny building was far too small to house the hundreds who had come. Candles shed a rosy glow through the open doorways, the monotonous droning of the voice of Father S was joined by that of his son, also in the priesthood, while a choir of six sang the chants. Father S's son is an exact replica of his father, except that his beard is jet black.

The church has been dedicated to the Prophet Elijah. No more hurling of sheds down hillsides should be necessary now. The Prophet must be well pleased with his church; even the doubting Nicos took part in its construction. He showed us with pride the low wall he had helped to build that skirts the church porch.

After the service, a somewhat incongruous entertainment, a fair, had been set up on level ground below the newly consecrated church. Stalls of cheap plastic toys, fancy hats, plaster busts of Aphrodite and other gods and goddesses and sticky sweets vied with each other to be taken home by some undiscerning customer. Among the sweets were long brown sticks of *soutsouko*, a Cyprus favourite, made from whole almonds set in what can only be described as a rubber-like substance made from grape juice and flour. A small boy, knee high to a grasshopper, staged a small temper tantrum until his tired father gave in and gave him what he wanted, a vicious-looking Kalashnikov made from black and yellow plastic.

The evening sky hung crimson and gold above us, the little church sparkled like a bright star on its high hill and the mountains receded into evening in waves of prussian blue, violet and indigo, as we all wended our several ways homewards. For once, the bumpy old mountain track was choked with traffic.

Dearest Ma,

I am reading Montaigne's *Essays*. He says that it is surely much better to be *wise* rather than *learned*. He quotes the fates of Aristotle and Varro, both men bursting at the seams with learning and both utterly miserable. However, I do wish I had an ability to learn languages, especially now with Greek, as it would enhance village conversation wonderfully. My attempts at the Greek evening classes in Larnaca were disastrous, partly but only partly because I started them halfway through the term and everyone else seemed to have grasped a certain amount. The fact that most of the class was half my age did

127

not add to one's confidence. Here are samples from a phrase book I took up during siesta time today. Where shall we start? Ah yes.

A Visit:

'I bring you a letter of recommendation' is the first phrase suggested, a sort of opening gambit. Next comes 'My friend John (or other) begs you for help.' As this will hardly help my visits to Old Crystalla or to Old Kemon and Maria and others, I read on. 'He will be faithful to you', the book assures me, and my reply could well be 'I shall do my best for him because he is a good man!'

It is not surprising that my book leaves out all feminine references, but I plough on.

Expressions of Admiration and Surprise:

'Ah, what an excellent view!' I say to my prospective Greek friend, while after he (or she) nods agreement, I could continue with: 'I am not satiated to look the beauty around me', or alternately, 'All is wonderful!' Perhaps I can try out these expressions on the goats and pigs in the dress circle up the mountains and these exchanges could enliven one's daily constitutionals.

I try again; with a view to chatting up those at our village hotel.

Arriving at the Hotel:

'Here we are, sir. We arrived at the hotel.'
'Shall I see you orderly?' I reply.
Either of us then might say: 'Please, get off!'
Then entering the hotel I say: 'Good evening, sir. I want an one bedroom.'

The porter now gets either helpful or bossy. 'Arrange your luggages, sir,' says he.

I retaliate by saying to no one in particular: 'Close the wireless.'

Are you having gold autumn days? I can hear the currawongs calling in the evening.

All love

L

Monday

Visitors are still arriving. Fortunately the more awkward of them prefer to stay at Anna's hotel rather than risking life with us.

Angus and Cyril have flown off. Their one-week holiday has not been an unqualified success. This opinion appears to be more or less universal. Before their departure for the airport Cyril was much fussed with last-minute arrangements but Angus sat heavily in the hotel foyer muttering sadly to himself, 'It's all very muddling. I don't know. I suppose we'll get there in one piece.'

It was with relief that we noted Cyril unearthing the mislaid plane tickets from Angus's rucksack, an incongruous piece of equipment for an ex-banker, man-about-town and celebrated financier. Equally incongruous is his shiny orange and chocolate sweatshirt, his safari trousers with pockets up and down both legs (never in danger of fleeing from an elephant) and his chunky black and white trainers. The prospect of being obliged to look after the pair of them for a moment longer, should the tickets not be found, was alarming. Once the tickets were dug from the bottom of the rucksack, Cyril was sent off upstairs for Angus' missing cigarettes and then hurried out to negotiate the taxi fare with Leonides (he of the sexy leather jacket).

'Try flying to Australia,' I tease Angus as his expression grew more and more distrait. 'Then you would know what flying is.'

129

By the end of his holiday Angus' pomposity had settled into a rather pathetic lostness of soul. Once out of Britain, he seemed to lose all confidence in himself as an Englishman of Substance and allowed the foreignness of his surroundings to conquer his morale. His response was to drown his sorrows in Scotch.

'I'm an alcoholic by profession,' he announced rather suddenly at our first meeting. This made me very nervous, as the pair had accepted an invitation to dinner here and I advised Tim to watch the situation closely.

'Can you take the boys to Nicosia tomorrow to collect their hire car?' Tim asked me the day after their arrival. To refer to the pair as 'boys' seemed a little over the top. As usual, Tim was at his office and too busy to help, but I was softened up by being reminded that Angus had offered to take us all to lunch at the Hilton. The invitation included our elderly friend Lady Cordelia, who has been staying with us. In addition, two high-powered Cypriot lawyers were to attend. Tim promised not to be late and to keep an eye on the bottles.

By some miracle we managed to keep Angus sober during lunch, urging him to nibble on avocado and chicken salad and a fairly filling bread roll. However, a certain amount of alcohol did manage to reach his grey matter and during a lull in the conversation he was heard to say crossly, 'That is the third time you have asked me what school I went to.' Dear Cordelia apologized profusely and Angus, not hearing her, concluded, 'But I won't tell you how long ago that was. Probably before Osbet Wilde!'

'Oscar,' someone said.

'Osbert Wilde. Great actor, that chap, what?'

Fortunately the two lawyers had to rush off at this point and said their goodbyes. Whether or not they had heard of Osbert Wilde ceased to matter. Tim took Cordelia off to show her his office while I was left with 'the two boys'.

We made for the hire car place somewhere near the old Venetian walls. We collected the car without too much difficulty: a bright purple creation, but a bit small for Angus' bulk. Somehow we got him wedged into the back, me manoeuvring his feet while Cyril steered his head. Cyril explained he would be more comfortable there. One could see what he meant as Angus' head lolled backwards and several stentorian snores issued forth.

'Follow me,' I said to Cyril, not much liking the look of him either, and steered my Mazda into the mêlée of rush hour traffic. However, the purple car stalled every few minutes and long queues began building up behind us. We drove in stately procession, Cyril indifferent to the frantic honking of tired commuters and refusing to quicken his pace, while Angus remained unconscious in the back. Stopping and starting half a dozen times, we at length reached the open road and, noting that the purple car was still in view in my rear mirror, I felt confident in accelerating to eighty kilometres an hour. Very soon there was no sign of Cyril. I slowed down and the purple car edged once more into my rear mirror. I accelerated again, cautiously. The purple car vanished. We were now on the motorway and this situation repeated itself for some twenty kilometres while other vehicles roared past us in increasing numbers. Finally, pulling on to the hard shoulder, I switched off the engine. Cyril appeared again, parked behind and got out. Moving with care, he approached my car and leant an elbow on my window sill, his face barely six inches from mine. He explained in measured tones that the hire car could not do more than fifty-five kilometres an hour 'as it was new'. The gears were 'sticky'. He would adjust them in the morning.

Forbearing to say that very likely more than the gears needed adjusting, I started my car and we soldiered on.

During the week that followed we arranged, rather optimistically, lunch at a favourite Larnaca seafood restaurant to be followed by a visit to Kolossi Castle, once the home of the Knights Templar. However, it soon became apparent that the castle visit was 'off', the restaurant lunch having left Angus very much the worse for wear. This was a pity in more ways than one, for we had an English friend staying who was keen to go and, in addition, the castle is the birthplace of the famous Commandaria wine invented

by the Knights and still very much in demand. On reflection, forgoing a visit here could have been a good move, all things considered.

As we waved the pair off to the airport on the day of their departure, I tackled Tim. Why had this extraordinary couple come here?

'Angus knows everybody who is anybody. He will arrange for Andreas' company to get listed on the London Stock Exchange. He is very influential.'

'Golly,' I said.

SEPTEMBER

Tuesday

A fine powdery dust hangs over the landscape. Even the dark green of the carob trees has turned a ghostly colour. The first oleanders are out to greet us on our return from our summer break in England. They bloom in rose, pink and white along the carriageways and up the mountainsides, but everywhere the brown land cries out for water. Cool, clear water! The sky seems flatter as the heat mounts, and the white walls of our courtyard dazzle the eye and the senses. A languor hangs over village and countryside and the women's chatter is soft and subdued.

We stopped on our way home at our favourite supermarket at Larnaca, our purpose to get some fresh fish fillets, a little meat, English biscuits and French jam. An early visit to our village butcher's shop on our arrival here several years ago tested my sensibilities to their limits, as well as my knowledge of the language. Maria had offered to escort me a second time but I declined her offer as graciously as I could. Much as we wish to patronize our village suppliers (and do), there is something infinitely reassuring about neat rows of recognizable objects, a cheerful clean assistant (who tells me he is soon to start up a butcher's shop in Albania), and no obligation to point at a grinning carcass or to make suitable noises to identify a particular animal. The fruit and veg up the mountain is always fresh and plentiful and two small general stores supply much else, one of them sending a truck full of fruit, veg and tinned stuff twice a day to our village down the hill. Wishing to show solidarity with the locals, we tried our luck with the local bread at first, but the giant flying saucers were stale by the time we were a quarter of the way through. The quality of the local wines, so enjoyed by Richard the Lionheart, continues to thrill, as does the excellent brandy and vodka. Cyprus wines are also given a good press in The Song of Solomon.

134

We paid a visit to Lambros this afternoon. His plant nursery is in the lowlands and he labours under what are becoming more and more trying conditions. Lambros has two wells, served by underground springs. These water his vineyard and several acres of trees as well as his bedding plants. One well is now dry, the second is low. As we sip the strong sweet coffee in his bachelor parlour (his wife has departed), Lambros's usually cheerful optimism is waning. I tell him about the droughts my grandfather knew in Central Queensland, the first lasting from the moment my grandfather brought his young bride up from Melbourne until three years later. My mother would tell us of her parents' first home, a wooden house with a corrugated iron roof and wide verandahs 'that floated in a sea of dust'. The whole experience was a ghastly shock for my poor grandmother, who had been brought up in an entrancing world of balls, theatres, family theatricals and musical soirées. The latter were held at the family home every Sunday evening. Here her parents entertained the socialites of Melbourne, in particular the bohemian set, which my Irish great-grandfather clasped fondly to his romantic Celtic bosom. Here he sang duets with Nellie Melba and entertained Clara Butt and the parents of Percy Grainger.

Apart from floating in a sea of dust, my grandparents' home was parked in the middle of the featureless plains near Longreach. 'Look at the hill,' the growing family would shriek as this strange phenomenon appeared on the thirty-mile drive into town. Their sheep station was one hundred thousand acres in size, the nearest neighbour some thirty miles away. There was a Chinese cook and a Chinese gardener. The former kept the food fresh in a Kalgoolie safe made from hessian soaked in a tray of water. In a good season the Chinese gardener grew vegetables. During droughts the bath water was given to the last milking cow. (No soap could be used.) When the first rain fell and began drumming on the tin roof, my three-year-old aunt shrieked with fright.

But Lambros was not diverted by my tales. Who could blame him? He could see no relevance in swapping drought stories in a

135

land so far away and at a time so long ago. We bought several clay pots as we departed, not so much for our own needs as for his. We would have liked to have bought more. Lambros works so hard, assisted by one woman, a Filipina, who he says can be relied on to work as hard as he does. All he needs is rain. As our car pulled out of his yard we could see him scanning the horizons for the first wisp of autumn cloud, his weather-beaten features creased with care.

Friday

Old Crystalla has been given a pacemaker. She had a heart attack in August when we were abroad. She is down on the coast convalescing with her daughter, Maroulla. Old Demetri, meanwhile, manages to get a lift up here every day in a friend's truck. However, there have been one or two days lately when he has not appeared. Noticing the hens had a distracted, restless look about them today, and his grey and white cat kept mewing at our door, I decided to see about their breakfasts. I have been made privy to the secret niche where Demetri keeps the key to his store room. It is hardly secret as anyone passing his yard can spot it without difficulty. Unlocking the door, I went inside to investigate. At one end of the shed the now defunct remnants of domestic life stretching over many decades are piled ceiling high. On the walls hang reminders of the family's life of ceaseless toil, some of these items still in use. There are the usual hand-made implements – a sickle, a yoke for oxen of beaten metal and stitched cloth padding, panniers of woven cane lined with goatskin, crudely stitched, farm tools of various shapes and sizes. (A heavy wooden hand plough which is still pulled by Madonna is propped against the shed outside.) On the floor are sacks of grain, potatoes and carob pods. I rummaged about in the darkness and settled finally on what I hope was a sack of crushed corn. It made up into a strange greyish mash when I added water and I then poured it into the hens' feeding trays. On reflection, I am hoping the mixture wasn't cement, where the term egg-bound could have unfortunate connotations. Crystalla's white doves hovered about hoping to have a share of the leftovers.

Next I went down to the fields to check on Madonna. She was looking indignant and her braying had grown exasperated. She had eaten every morsel she could find within the restricted area of her field. I struggled to remove the iron stake that held her tethering rope but Old Demetri had skewered it so firmly to a giant elder flower root, it could not be budged. I tried to remove her rope halter but the piece of chain beneath her lower jaw had been looped into a slip knot that had tightened uncomfortably as she strained upon it. The grey and white cat appeared, mewing its hunger. Madonna flattened her ears in disapproval and did a quick charge. The cat leapt over a fennel and retreated. I managed to release the slip knot a little and Madonna relaxed. She sniffed in my pocket for the piece of bread.

'I'll get you some water,' I told her. Where was Old Demetri? I found a bucket in the courtyard and slopped my way downhill. Madonna sniffed at the bucket, knocking it over.

'*Kalimera!*' One of the villagers passed, en route to his plot.

'I am worried about the donkey. For two days she has had no water,' I called.

'*Endaksi. Endaksi!* She OK.'

'Are you sure?'

'*Ne. Ne.* Don't worry.'

Perhaps donkeys are like camels.

Next I went to deal with the grey and white cat.

OCTOBER

Two grandsons have just been packed off home to Britain after a strenuous week. After agreeing to pay for a course in scuba-diving for each of them, I had a rude shock when I discovered the cost. However, as grandparents are expected to distribute largesse no matter if the tally of grandchildren has reached seven, I arranged the bookings and on Day One we three set off for the coast. The boys donned their gear with suppressed excitement and with everything strapped on and climbed into, they looked more like creatures from outer space as they followed their instructor, first into a swimming pool for some underwater breathing practice and then across the sand and into a rather shallow, somewhat murky stretch of sea. Why, I wondered, didn't this scuba-diving school choose some of this island's lovely coves rather than this particular spot? But Ben and Matthew were more than satisfied, doing their homework from their manuals with an enthusiasm I doubt they employ with homework back home. At the end of the week they passed their exams with flying colours and were complimented by their instructor for their hard work, dedication – and excellent manners! Where will they practise their new skills in the UK? In an empty quarry, someone said.

Sunday

The island lies under a pall of heat. The sheets on our bed feel as though they have just been ironed. Our air conditioners purr away and partly cancel out the barking of the dogs, so that in spite of everything we can get some sleep. We feel sorry for the dogs, who are riding out another summer in their dusty pens in the airless valley.

We go to our favourite little bay to cool off in the early morning, Tim bathing, standing up to his waist. He is a bit of a cowardy custard. The sea is aquamarine, the water as clear as lemonade. Cliffs the colour of clotted cream rise up from the water, doubling their images below. However, up on these cliffs Costas' twenty-cent shower outside the taverna is out of action. Water is, as usual, in short supply. After our cool drinks on his terrace, we drive home, salted all over like herrings.

The wretched shooting season is under way. The dogs have sniffed it coming for some weeks, their barking louder and more hysterical than ever. For a while we thought we had won the battle with the two next door. However, to our dismay, two new dogs seem to have replaced the former two, who were spirited away after Tim's strong-man approach some months back. This had involved another visit by the mukhtar in the company of our two local policemen, plus Tim and me. The two policemen, who live pleasantly peaceful lives in their quarters up the hill, had seemed unprepared for the reception that our neighbour's wife had ready for them. Stepping aside to let her deal with the matter, her burly husband had retreated in a rather cowardly fashion towards the house. His wife laid into the two upholders of the law with a startling disregard for their authority or that of the mukhtar himself. The dogs in question grew silent, straining and panting in their wire cages in solidarity with their owners. As the conversation, mostly one way, was all in Greek, Tim and I stood by, feeling rather foolish. The mukhtar said little, trying to look affable as our neighbour's wife grew shriller and shriller. A pink flush on her throat and bosom deepened as she warmed to her task. Every time one or other of the young men attempted to remonstrate, they were beaten into submission. At last it seemed pointless to carry on and with a few nods and hand shakes we left, while the mukhtar strode back to his coffee house and the policemen returned to their car. As our party broke up, the two dogs set up a barrage of barking that set the hillsides ringing. However, some days later their barking had fizzled out and for three months or so there has been peace and quiet over the way. Now we are back to square one!

Today being one of the two shooting days of the week – the other is Wednesday – the noise from the kennels starts well before dawn, when the hunters gather the dogs together and then make for The House of the Wind for Thekla's energizing breakfast. By the time the sun has risen over the sea yonder, our braves are out on the hills, blasting at everything that moves. The loud reports from the guns, one bang or a series of bangs, alternate with or drown out the voice of Father S and his chanters, or else vie with the pealing of the bells. To be attending church on a winter's morning can be a disconcerting experience.

This afternoon, a series of startlingly loud reports sent me catapulting from my siesta to peer from our bedroom window. As I looked across Demetri's flat rooftop, I was rewarded with the spectacle of a bunch of white feathers exploding in mid air and then gently drifting earthwards. The doves! They had shot one of Old Crystalla's white doves! I called to Tim, who went off to investigate.

'For heaven's sake, don't get shot!'

There was a case, reported in the papers recently, of a villager caught napping under a tree. As he stood up to protest his innocence, he was greeted with a faceful of gunshot and had to be flown to England for treatment. Hope was expressed that one of his eyes could be saved.

I telephoned Maroulla to give the message about the dove to her mother. She and her parents were out but a grand-daughter promised to pass it on. Tim returned home to say that he had remonstrated with the hunters who were prowling around Old Demetri's orchard.

'They have apologized,' said Tim. 'They say they won't come so close to the village again.'

'Did you spot any locals?'

'I couldn't tell.' Tim lied. 'They were all wearing hats.'

He produced a handful of spent cartridges.

'These were lying outside the orchard, in the lane. I'll keep them as evidence.'

We went back together, taking our camera. There were more feathers on the paving stones of Old Demetri's garden. A white object caught my eye on the storeroom roof.

'That's only a plastic bag,' said Tim. 'I noticed it before.'

'No, it isn't. It's far too white for a plastic bag. It's a dove!'

Tim fetched a rickety, home-made ladder that was nearby and propped it against the storeroom wall, avoiding the nettles that grow thigh high. He retrieved the poor dead creature, which lay warm and still in his hand. Not a trace of blood marked its pristine whiteness but the bird was decidedly dead. How many others were gone, we wondered? Their gentle billing and cooing each morning provides a welcome contrast to the more strident wake-up calls of Demetri's rooster and to Madonna's soulful braying. We searched about but could see no sign of the other doves, dead or alive.

I had noticed the jungle-green clad figure of Evagora's son, Marcos, slinking homewards along our lane shortly after the flying feathers incident. With his gun broken across his arm and his hurrying gait, he presented a decidedly guilty appearance.

I was undecided what to do. A high state of indignation is not the right moment for following up culprits. However, at that moment, Andreas emerged from next door on his way to his farm. I showed him the feathers and cartridges; Tim meanwhile had left on some errand with the dead bird. Turning on his heel, Andreas disappeared indoors again. There followed a number of sounds: Andreas' deep voice raised in anger, the husky voice of his son and Evagora's shrill excited defence of her boy.

Half an hour later Andreas, with a face of thunder, got into his truck, while Evagora knocked on our door. She was holding a small plate with something on it wrapped in silver foil.

'My son wants you to have this cheese. You do like *halumi*, don't you? He makes it himself on his farm. It is very nice if you grill it the way we do in Cyprus. You know why it is so good, don't you? Because we feed our goats on thyme. That is why.'

'Thanks very much, Evagora. Please thank Marcos.'

141

'He wants me to tell you he is very sorry. My husband has given him a thrashing. The poor boy! He won't do it again.'

'You know, Evagora, it is illegal for hunters to come within four hundred metres of a village. It was frightening. They were right in the lane by Demetri's house!'

'Were they?' asked Evagora, all innocence.

Monday

Tim has made a fly trap which he has hung on the grape trellis. It contains a liquid of such obnoxious aroma we are unable to approach within yards of the thing for the first few days of its replenishment. The smell has the opposite effect on the flies, who just love it. He has also painted the ugly cement floor of the courtyard a smart yellow ochre. The powder-blue flowers of our plumbago go very nicely with it. The painting operation took him days, bent on all fours with his paintbrush, while I rushed to and fro with iced tea or fresh lime juice to keep the worker from dehydration.

We are amused by the fly traps that are popular in local tavernas: bags of clear plastic filled with water that hang from the trees. A proprietor the other day, questioned as to their usefulness, explained that the flies see themselves reflected there and, narcissus-like, fall in love with their reflections. What happens next is not clear. The results are not impressive.

Wednesday

Marcos has sold his goats. They do not earn him enough to help him pay off the seven-hundred-pound loan on his new car. His dusty, decrepit truck is on its very last legs and besides, all eligible young men, if they wish to remain eligible, must own a car.

He sat in our front parlour this morning while I offered coffee and sympathy.

143

'How many did you have, Marcos?'

'One hundred and fifty,' Evagora offered, poking her head in the door. 'He loved his goats!'

Marcos stared disconsolately at his boots. 'I like my goats too much,' he said.

'I'm really sorry to hear about this. I mean, that you've had to sell them. Could you not find some extra work to help with the overdraft?'

'No,' replied his mother, sticking her head through the door again, as she finished attaching her hose for watering the sheep to the communal water tap in the lane. 'He must look after the goats all the time. You can't just leave them! Now he has got a job but it is only for two weeks. He was so happy with his goats! He didn't want any other life than that.'

Evagora sighed. We all felt sad. Marcos, his dark eyes as expressive as his mother's, rose heavily to his feet. Declining a second cup of coffee, he went out, his workmen's boots clonking on the tiled floor, his powerful frame sagging.

The Cypriot's fondness for the goat, 'this insatiable rodent', as an exasperated British administrator once called the animal, together with heavy tree felling, helped to change the island's character – and its climate – once and for all.

Cyprus was once covered in marvellous forests, which survived the demands for shipbuilding in ancient times. But herds of goats wandered the forests, nibbling at new growth to such an extent that regeneration was impossible. In addition to the havoc this caused, the local population hacked and burned the forests for arable land, exploited the best trees to obtain sap and pitch, firewood or bark for the tanneries. But the goats did their work. In order to avoid exploitative taxation, the locals found that keeping their goats hidden in the forests was an effective ploy. The British, after occupying Cyprus in 1878, passed a special 'Goat Law' banning goats from the most important forests. But still the locals took persuading. A major breakthrough occurred in the 1930s when the powerful monasteries gave up their right to pasture in the forests. A whole series of villages was bribed to move down to the coastal plains, where they were given free houses and land and presumably permission to keep goats. The British left behind forests that covered nineteen per cent of the island. However, in the political troubles of 1964 and 1974 large areas of these precious forests went up in flames. The Turkish invasion of 1974 led to the destruction of sixteen per cent of state-owned forests in the north. Today, all over Cyprus, terraces which have been barren for decades are being replanted with trees – and forests bring rain!

But now that Marcos' goats have gone, who will make us fresh *halumi*?

Thursday

My cousin Rosemary arrived from Sydney today. By some mischance, hard to comprehend when one considers the homely dimensions of Larnaca's airport, we missed each other. While I read a newspaper on a bench just outside the Arrivals area, Rosemary was wandering about getting crosser and crosser with a cousin who had failed to turn up. At last, within less than a coo-ee distance, we spotted each other with shrieks of relief. I drove her to our village hotel, where she has expressed the wish to spend her week. News of the midges, which seem to breed promiscuously in our bougainvillaea, and the dogs, seems to have penetrated even to the Antipodes. At the hotel Rosemary was restored to her usual good humour by some local wine and the charm of her room, vacated a year ago by cousin Roz. I left her to unpack in peace, promising her a store of Cypriot delights if not a feisty lawyer from the Balkans.

Sunday

An invitation to visit the Occupied North came unexpectedly last

145

week. Tim and I have contemplated going on a number of occasions but are aware that Greek Cypriot relatives of 'The Disappeared' picket the border crossing from time to time. We respect their attitude. However, curiosity to discover a little of how the other half lives got the better of me and when I had a phone call from my Australian friend Mary last week, I accepted her invitation readily. Mary is also visiting from Sydney. She will collect Rosemary and me in a friend's car at 7 a.m. sharp tomorrow.

Monday

Mary collected us punctually, and we bowled up the carriageway to Nicosia in the black Mercedes, the glorious early morning light dappling the brown landscape and the sad and dusty eucalyptus in the gulleys. Why don't Cypriot gums smell as sweet as the Australian ones? They grow more lushly here when given half a chance and do not have the diseases that our myriads of wild birds often spread. But they lack those heady scents. As we approached Nicosia in the early light, the strange chalk hills skirting the city glowed in shades of dusty pink.

At the Ledra Palace border crossing with its barbed wire barricades and sobering UN presence, we parked the car on the 'Greek' side and passed through to the Turkish officials at passport control. This was in a small, badly ventilated building set in a dusty yard. Giant gums bordering the compound were a reassuring sight: Nature knows no frontiers. However, this, for Mary, was unfriendly territory. We paid for our visas and filled in a detailed questionnaire about our proposed route and plans for the day. The Turkish official found my Australian passport and Rosemary's of little interest and handed them back with a nod. Passport controls have given me the jitters ever since the day I inadvertently travelled from London to Rome on my daughter Phoebe's passport. She was then aged twelve. By some miracle I made it, thanks to a slow-witted official at Heathrow who gave me a funny look. A sleepy official in Rome was more interested in promoting a friend's taxi service into the city than doing his job and once more I was let through, but the experience was unnerving.

The Turkish official turned to Mary. 'You say you are Italian?' 'That's right,' replied my friend, all charm and prettiness. 'But you have a Greek name!' He did not smile back. 'My husband is Greek but I am Australian. I was born there, as you can see. There are many Italians in Australia.'

Her coolness was commendable. A twenty-year dream hung in the balance. I attempted a diverting, supportive smile but her interrogator was concentrating all his visual and mental powers on Mary. While she sparkled and beamed, he was dealing with an internal struggle that lasted some minutes. He studied her passport from cover to cover, frowning. All three of us (and no doubt the Turk) knew that Mary possessed not one drop of Italian blood. We also knew that only a Greek with rare and pressing reasons to do so can cross into the north, under certain conditions, and vice-versa. 'Only diplomats, UN soldiers and foreigners may enter freely' says our guide book.

There was a policeman, by chance an Australian, standing nearby. He tried to look friendly yet non-committal. For a few agonizing moments our cause looked dicey.

'Very well. But you will report back here by six p.m.'

While we waited for a taxi, the Australian policeman chatted us up. He was on a two-year assignment from Canberra, he said. He asked us where we were going and eagerly Mary unfolded her map. It was a fatal move.

'You will not go there!'

A hairy finger jabbed at our map, its owner wearing a most unpromising expression. 'You will go *here* and *here*! That is all!' The Turkish official glowered.

That left us with Turkish Nicosia, Famagusta, Salamis and Kyrenia but not the main target of our visit, Mary's bridal village! It lay not far from Famagusta and she had found it on the map. The Turkish policeman waved us impatiently into our taxi while

147

our Australian melted into the background. Mary took her disappointment with stoicism.

Our driver introduced himself as Ahmed. As our journey progressed, bumping along in the burgeoning heat in his clapped out taxi, he thawed a little. Just a little. He expressed regret that the life of the old days had gone. It was better, he said, when Cyprus was a united country, when Turk and Greek lived in harmony together.

Ahmed took us first to the thirteenth-century cathedral of St Sophia, converted into the Selimiye mosque by the invading Ottomans in the sixteenth century. Two incongruous minarets replace the original steeples. This Turkish part of Nicosia has preserved much of its ancient past, whereas Greek Nicosia, which the Greeks call Lefkosia, has all but bulldozed its heritage out of existence.

On we hurried to Famagusta, the city of ghosts on its beautiful bay. Founded in the third century BC by Ptolemy II, it is still known to the Greeks as Amochostos. With the fall of Acre in 1291, the city grew and flourished as a centre for East–West trade. Here the jewellery of a merchant's daughter was said to be 'worth more than that of the Queen of France' and loose women were the 'most expensive in the world'. But the city's wealth was its undoing. A particularly obnoxious invader, named Lala Mustafa, tortured to death the Venetian commander in charge of the city (breaking a promise to spare his life). He then drove out the Christians or had them all murdered, while requisitioning the de Lusignans' cathedral as a mosque. Known now as the Lala Mustafa mosque, it is, or was, a masterpiece of Gothic architecture, somewhat incongruous in its location on the fringes of the Orient. We left our shoes outside and went into the bare cool interior. Quotes from the Koran hang from the walls, the fluted columns are painted white, and prayer mats cover the old tombstones on the floors.

With the heat of the day rising, we bought ourselves some cool drinks to slake our growing thirst. These and some postcards were more or less all that the Greek Cypriot government would allow us in the way of purchases. As we left Famagusta, we tried to picture the frantic scenes as thirty thousand of its residents fled the Turkish tanks and bombs in 1974. A total of one hundred and fifty thousand Greek Cypriots fled to the south, and many of their villages are still empty. Greek Cypriots such as my artist friend Maria have yet to receive compensation for their losses.

'There's my village!' Mary pointed excitedly. 'Oh *please* slow down, Ahmed! Can't you take us there? I'll pay you extra!'

Ahmed did not slow down. He was unhappy but he could not stop. 'I will lose my job,' he told us. 'They watch us all the time. They know where I am taking you. They know *everything*!'

All too soon Mary's village began receding over to the left of us, its church tower and minaret growing fainter and fainter on the skyline. Mary, after her initial dismay, grew philosophical.

'I'll come back. You'll see. I'll be back and I'll try again. I was married in that village! Both my kids were born there.'

Ahmed's shoulders sagged, his whole body sagged but he drove steadily on. All of us felt wretched. To come twelve thousand miles for this!

'When the Turks invaded and the tanks came, I just had time to grab the kids and jump into the car. It was so unreal. A Turkish soldier knocked on our door. He was very polite but I didn't wait for explanations. All I could remember at the time was wondering why he had bothered to knock.'

'Where did you go?'

'South. The British had a base at Dhekelia which they set up as a refugee camp. My husband found us there. We lived on mince for a month! Luckily I'd bought some clean nappies for the baby. Nothing else.' When it became clear that their home and their way of life was lost, Mary and her family finally left for Australia.

Ahmed took us next to Salamis. If our frustration needed a further boost, we got it here in this ancient capital. Barely had we time to tread a few ruins, peer into the odd Roman steam

149

bath or plonk our bottoms on a stone seat in the old amphitheatre (which once seated some fifteen thousand souls), than our guide was beckoning us on. Not, however, before we were able to examine an ancient Roman wc with flushing gutters and seating for forty-four persons! Do you not know, Ahmed, that here in beautiful Salamis, King Koullas I (411–374 BC) united Cyprus for the first time in its history? That he brought art, commerce, culture and prosperity? Here in Salamis, Barnabas the Jew was born. He was brought up in Jerusalem, where he was converted to Christianity. And to Salamis he returned in AD 45, accompanied by Paul, visiting synagogues but not pagan temples. Which route did he and Paul take to Paphos, on the far south-west of the island? This journey was probably as new to Barnabas as it was to Paul, for they had to hack their way through thick forests, even on the plains, yet they spent but ten days on the island. In Acts we read of Paul's new powers: when in Paphos he struck blind the Jewish magician Elymas for expressing anti-Christian views. This greatly impressed the Roman Proconsul, Sergius Paulus. After this visit Paul gave up the name Saul and took the Roman one of Paul.

Unfortunately, Barnabas fell out with Paul but returned to Cyprus seven years later, this time with Mark. It was a tragic homecoming, for he was burnt at the stake in Salamis. A handwritten copy of St Matthew's Gospel was buried with him.

On we drove, on across the stark and dusty Mesaoria Plain, the site of Richard the Lionheart's decisive battle against King Issac. In 1330 the plain became a vast lake when heavy rain flooded Nicosia. Where are the trees, the orchards and crops that bloomed before 1974, we asked Ahmed. The Turks let them die.

There was a short break to allow us to scramble up the ramparts of St Hilarion, the crusader castle perched on dizzy heights above the harbour town of Kyrenia. Although it was built as one of a chain of fortresses running all the way to Syria, we learnt that our old friends the Lusignan family used it later as a summer palace. The castle is approached through a grove of pines, and

151

wedged between two great crags. They must have had well-developed leg muscles, or perhaps they were carried up in litters? What a view! On a clear day you can see the mountains of Turkey, forty miles distant. Angels in flight must have marvelled.

To get to the castle we passed along a road running right through a Turkish army camp. Signs in several languages told us that stopping and taking photographs was strictly forbidden. However, once on the ruins of the ramparts, we could get an excellent view right across the camp.

A quick look at Kyrenia. It has a pretty harbour and was once a favourite spot for the international smart set. Then we bobbed into the small museum in the castle. Here we inspected a splendid wooden trading ship dating from Alexander the Great (300 BC). Cyprus, famous for its metal working, had provided Alexander with a sword much treasured for its lightness and quality. In the boat were the bronze eating utensils and drinking cups and plates that the four crew had used. Rows of amphora were stacked on the deck; some had contained wine, oil and almonds. How strange to see almonds, still in their shells, after two thousand years under the sea!

All around Kyrenia harbour are the old carob warehouses, now converted into cafés and restaurants, though few visitors were about. Carobs were once known as 'the black gold of Cyprus'. We lunched at Bellapais, there being some difference of local opinion as to which of two particular trees was Lawrence Durrell's Tree of Idleness. Convinced by the Turkish proprietor of our little tavern that we were, indeed, under the said tree, we ate our lunch of kebabs, salads and pitta bread.

The old Gothic abbey of Bellapais lies in ruins above the cliffs that run down to the harbour. The name is a corruption of Abbaye de la Pais. In the good old days the Lusignan King Hugo III granted the monks of the abbey the privilege of 'riding with a gilded sword and golden spurs'. No cold baths and bread and dripping for them. They lived like princes and a contemporary observer noted that not only did each have one wife but several.

152

These Premonstratensian monks dressed in white, the abbey being known as the white abbey. However, all good things come to an end and during the period of the Venetian rulers (1489–1571) Cyprus fell under a dark period, the Cypriot population became little better than slaves and the abbey fell into disrepair. Its ruin was completed when the Ottomans invaded in 1571.

Today, another exodus, that of 1974, is painfully evident in the abbey church, where a dusty Bible still lies open on the lectern and decaying prayer books lie along the pews. A hideous concrete monument not far off celebrates the 'Turkish Peace Operation', the invasion of the north on 20th July 1974. Captured Greek tanks decorate the environs.

Ahmed made sure we reported back to the border guards sharp at 6 p.m.

'I'll come back,' Mary told him. 'Who knows? Next time our island may be free!'

Ahmed, looking Mary in the eye at last, gave a sad, unhopeful smile.

Wednesday

Today Koulla was picking leaves off the mulberry tree near the car park.

'*Ella,*' she said.

So I followed her into her house, where she demonstrated how she soaks her jars of fresh olives in brine with the mulberry leaves. After eight days she will remove the leaves and the result is *poli kala.*

Friday

On my early morning walk today I met Panicos striding along with two long sticks cut and pared from oleander branches. He

154

is a powerfully built young man. He informed me that he was on his way to his almond trees as the nuts are now ready for harvesting.

'But you have nothing to put them in,' I pointed out. 'How will you collect them?'

'My mother will come,' Panicos replied. 'With a bucket.' This explanation seemed to satisfy him for a moment, until he thought of something to add to it. 'A bucket is good,' he said, 'as it has a handle.'

Does his mother have a handle as well, I wondered? One only has to look at her feet as the poor old soul waddles painfully about, to see that there is a certain injustice in this arrangement. Evanthia is deft with her hands, which, unlike her feet and her knees, behave the way she wants them to. Her lacework is some of the finest in the village. The tablecloth, kept in a large cardboard box when Evanthia is otherwise occupied, has taken her two and a half years to complete and is still not quite finished. It should be on display in a fine arts museum. But now she must gather up the almonds that her son is knocking off the trees. I am reminded of the old song 'He Holds the Candle While his Mother Chops the Wood'.

I pondered on all this as I pursued my walk and met Vassoula coming down the hill. She is visiting her parents, Old Kemon and Maria. She asked me if I would like to accompany her on a visit to the cemetery. I agreed and we set off, following the rough path down past the church. She explained that it is over a month since her arrival from the States for her annual visit, but with much work to do caring for her aged parents, she has had little time. Vassoula is the most faithful of the three daughters.

The sun was already warm on our backs. The dozen or so tall cypresses by the lychgate which, seen from our roof terrace in the early morning and evening, are an inky black, were now a dusty green. Dust hung in the air and in our nostrils, like incense. The winter rains have not yet begun.

'I wish to see the grave of my uncle,' Vassoula explained as we walked through the wooden door into the graveyard. We gazed about at the rows of dusty headstones beneath the dusty eucalyptus.

'When did your uncle die?'

'In January. My friends tell me his grave is the newest.'

We picked our way over the loose gravel and the tall dead grass. Vassoula stopped suddenly.

'Oh my God. Here is the father-in-law of my best friend!' We examined the inscription and the photograph of a man who had died sixteen years ago.

'How often do you come to the cemetery?' I asked, a trifle puzzled.

'I come every year, of course. Here is my neighbour. I remember her well. She was a very kind lady. And here, this one, this boy, he was only twelve years old!'

A fresh, smiling young face looked out from its headstone, into which his photograph had been set.

'This one. She is the mother of the priest. Oh my God. What can one do?'

I suggested we go further down and try to find the grave of her uncle. We found it, but it had no headstone. The withered flowers in their cellophane wrapping were still there although the little cards had been washed clean by last winter's rain.

'Yes, this must be the grave,' said Vassoula.

We stood in silence. At the end of the cemetery, part of its stone wall has been knocked down and loads of rubbish tossed inside. Two imposing tombs, much larger than all the rest, dominate the graveyard.

'That man,' Vassoula explained, pointing, 'he makes the tomb for his wife. They come back from New York and she die here. This man, he nearly goes crazy. He is having ribbons and lace and flowers everywhere and he is getting the priest to come and pray every day.'

I stared in dismay at the two marble edifices that had been erected with such care and expense. Both tombs look as though they have been trampled on by stampeding buffaloes. The eight elegant marble urns lie smashed to atoms. There is broken glass. An ugly cactus grows out of the tomb of the wife where the cracked marble slab has been wrenched away. Yet the owner had died two years after the Turkish invasion of the north, after the troubles that had heralded it.

'Who could have done all this damage?'

Vassoula shrugged. 'Maybe the dogs.'

We changed the subject and began our walk home.

'These orchards here, they are almonds and they belong to the church,' she explained. 'Every year there is an auction at the coffee shop. Whoever wins can sell them. Oh my God. There are many almonds!'

Some time ago, passing through one of the villages in the lowlands, Tim and I noticed a signpost to a Turkish cemetery. We left the road and parked our car beneath a grove of eucalypts and approached the fenced-off enclosure, entering the graveyard beneath a wrought iron archway. On the apex of this an emblem, also in wrought iron, served to warn the visitor of what lay within. This was the newest part of the cemetery. In the old part of the cemetery next door, surrounded by stone walls, the tombstones were quietly resting, shaded by trees. Here, everything was spare and stark. On our right we passed a row of rusting frames from

which the photographs of the dead had long since been wrenched out. Further on, facing us, two straight rows of tombstones, some two dozen in all, stood starkly on the parched ground. Each grave was identical and unmarked. Here was the proof of rumours we had heard, low-voiced rumours of 'a massacre'. The graves were separated from the main cemetery, the ghosts of the dead moving about in unhappy wanderings, never still, never at peace, while above the archway a dog howled at a crescent moon and dust blew...

NOVEMBER

Dearest Ma

At last we are getting some welcome rain after a very dry October. I do hope the drought in the west is easing? We get no news about Australia so our High Commissioner friend here supplies us with some now and again.

Up on our roof, Nicos (who I think I have told you about) is helping me stabilize the grape trellis. Some of the uprights are loose and the winter gales will soon be upon us. He brought some pieces of timber and did a fairly good job on the whole. At one place in the stone wall, however, the long nails sank into the plaster like a knife into butter.

'Do you think they will hold?'

'Yeah. No problem. If this piece here pulls away, Liz – when we get the big winds – you can ram that tub against it.' He pointed to one of my prized ceramic pots!

After he'd finished we had our mugs of tea and surveyed his handiwork. I told him about the poster that had been slipped under our door yesterday. Had he got one too? It showed the faces of four young men, clean-shaven and neatly dressed; four handsome young men of whom any mother would be proud. But the information beneath the photographs had dismayed us. The four young men had been executed by the British!

Nicos was sanguine. 'They were members of *Eoka*. They hung them. These things went on, y'know. Trouble on both sides, there was. Old Grivas, he was hiding out in those hills there for years.' He waved a hand.

I remember how Dad had disliked Grivas! And Makarios – 'that dishonest priest!'

'You see that derelict garden there?' Nicos said, jerking his head in the direction of the 'secret garden' over the way. An ancient wooden door in the wall hides the garden from street view, but up on our terrace we can look down upon the untidy rows of cylindrical ceramic beehives, the cracked flower pots, the trailing ivy and the weeds. Two loulloudia trees hang over it. The neighbourhood cats do their courting there.

'You see that?' continued Nicos nonchalantly. 'That place was an arsenal – grenades, guns, ammunition, you name it.'

Gratified at my reaction, he went on. 'See that road up there going past The House of the Wind? Well, they fired at a bus there, thought it was full of British soldiers! But it wasn't. The bus rolled down the hill and got stuck in a carob tree. You have to laugh.'

'Was anyone hurt?'

'Na. But gee, it must have been funny. Just local people in the bus, they were.'

'What I think *is* funny is that the people don't seem to resent us, the British,' I replied, conscious of how displeased Dad would have been at my disloyal remarks! 'They're all so friendly.'

'They're not a bad lot,' Nicos agreed. 'But I tell you this, Liz. You'll be bored out of y' mind if you settle here – everyone snoring their heads off by nine o'clock! Whatever made you come here, Liz? You need your head read, my girl.'

What other news is there?

Maria, who I've also told you about, has decided to close her little shop. The amount of time she has had to spend there does not justify itself, as the tourists have been spasmodic and penny-pinching.

'What is the matter with my prices, Leez? Do you think I am charging too much?'

'No. But one of the problems is your location. By the time the tourists reach your shop they have spent all their money, or else run out of time.'

Should I suggest to her that much of her produce is

160

impractical? Breakable ceramics and glassware are not the easiest of souvenirs to fly home in one's suitcase.

Maria will have to paint more pictures fast. She has an exhibition coming up in three months' time. And her cats, now numbering sixteen, are eating her out of house and home. I myself have not done much painting except one large oil (a landscape) and some designs for greeting cards. These show old men in the traditional baggy 'trousers', donkeys, churches and cypresses.

All love,

Libby

161

DECEMBER

Friday

Tim is not happy with his butch 'boss', though she is supposed to be a colleague, so to speak. Relations are strained and inclined to 'take the gilt off the gingerbread'. However, he soldiers on, aware that women's lib is here to stay.

Edmund is coming to us for Christmas. He will bring me some woolly tights I requested and his bag of tools. There are numerous jobs that are lined up for his expert attention.

The Cyprus Weekly reports today that a Greek Cypriot woman who received a favourable ruling last July against Turkey in the European Court of Human Rights is still awaiting damages. She was awarded six hundred and forty thousand pounds for loss of her property. Her battle has lasted six years. If Turkey continues to refuse to pay compensation for requisitioned property, the Council of Europe has threatened to expel it from its ranks. But will it? The Turks see this claim as the tip of the iceberg, so many Greek Cypriots having lost their possessions. The whole thing operates in reverse, of course. Maria, for instance, is occupying some Turkish chicken coops, while what has become of her family home in Famagusta remains a mystery. (The Turkish Cypriots tended to occupy the poorer quarters of these villages.)

Monday

Christmas has brought a nasty surprise. Busyness over preparations for the festive season has led me to spend less time than usual seeing to the lovebirds. So long as they are fed and watered and keep up their cheerful chatter, I am not aware that anything is amiss. However, the day before yesterday (the day Edmund arrived) I noticed a hole in the earthen floor of the aviary. This morning

162

there are only five little birds! There should be eight. There is no sign of Perky or his handsome blue and yellow son Claudius or his granddaughter, the shy and gentle Pandora. This is devastating. The four surviving children carry on as though nothing is wrong. They tended to find Perky a bossy father and grandfather, a chap who saw to it that they should give way in the pecking order. But poor Pinky is dazed and mute and far from being a merry widow.

Tim and Edmund have diagnosed rats! Too late in the season for snakes? At breakfast Tim had his suspicions confirmed when the head of a young rat emerged from the hole, its whiskers and pink nose twitching hungrily.

Both men have been hard at work all day. While Tim went off to buy yards of wire mesh from the do-it-yourself store down in the valley, Edmund started digging up one of the flower beds next to the aviary, through which the cunning rat parents have dug a tunnel some two metres long. That a dumb animal could think up such a clever strategy for getting free meals on tap is impressive. Not a feather of poor Perky or his children has been left as evidence! Only the sinister, gaping hole, now blocked off.

Tuesday

The men have been at work all day again. Strips of strong wire mesh have had to be laid low down in the flower bed and on the floor of the aviary, then weighted with heavy flat rocks. A back-breaking job for the chap in the aviary. This fell to poor Edmund, as he is somewhat shorter than Tim, and standing upright is impossible. To finish the job, they have laid doses of rat poison. We wish the rat family a merry Christmas.

Friday

After his sterling work on the rat problem, we felt that Edmund had earned a jaunt of some kind. The weather being particularly favourable yesterday and Christmas festivities over, we set off for the west coast. Past Limassol the road was empty and free and the blue-green sea and creamy rocks glittered in a wintery sun. We passed the British base at Episkopi with its beautiful green golf course edging the coastline, and after leaving Paphos (haven of the ex-pat) we turned north. Reckoning that we could 'do' Ayios Neophytos monastery before lunch, we headed for its serene portals where it nestles in a small steep valley. Here a micro climate allows tall moisture-loving plants to flourish in welcoming shades of green.

In 1159, a monk, later to become a Saint, settled into a cave in the tall rocks, cutting his home from the rock with his own hands. His wise sayings brought pilgrims flooding to the site so that, in order to maintain his hermit-like existence, he was forced to move higher up his rock. At the end of the century artists from Constantinople arrived to decorate his grotto with frescoes. These, with their stiff Byzantine faces and equally stiff clothing, still hold their original vibrant colour. Neophytos was alive and well when Richard the Lionheart stole the island from the King of Cyprus, the monk roundly condemning him for his barbarous conduct. The Monastery of Ayios Neophytos was established near the grotto in the sixteenth century. There is the loveliest garden here, sunk below ground level and enclosed by cloisters. The happy twittering of zebra finches, budgerigars and small African lovebirds enhances the contentment of the place. We met the monk in charge of the aviaries, Father Lucas, wearing his long black cassock and watering the plants. His voice is soft, his young face full of repose.

We ate lunch in a taverna right on the beach, well away from Paphos, where tourism has more or less cancelled out 'atmosphere'. We feasted on excellent calamari followed by a delicious white fish and *koupepia* (stuffed vine leaves). Although Cyprus is surrounded by sea, most fish served in restaurants is not caught locally and can be quite expensive. If Cyprus is accepted into the European Community in 2004, which seems likely, the cost of living will go up. Meanwhile we enjoy eating out and are making the most of it. Edmund and I finished up with a local dish, *loukoumia*, which though considered a speciality, was as bland as an English boarding house pudding – cubes of gelatin served in rosewater, with powdered sugar dusted on top. Tim, who eats like a sparrow, declined another course. A semi-dry white St Hilarion washed everything down nicely.

Somewhat languorous after our repast, we decided nevertheless to visit the ruins of ancient Paphos, destroyed not only by time but by several severe earthquakes.

Palæo Paphos was the centre of the worship of Aphrodite but the village of Kouklia and other developments now cover much of the site. Few cities in ancient times have been as glorified by the poets for their wealth and culture, and for great religious festivals. Sadly, now, little evidence remains as, apart from the earthquakes, much stonework was removed either by robbers or to build the other city, called Neo-Paphos. The old city is mentioned in The Acts of the Apostles and, being the residence of the proconsuls when under Roman rule, was the island's capital. We poked about among the ruins of the Great Temple, which Homer and others called the most revered temple in the world. Enormous stone blocks stand up, backed by the blue of the sea, and in its heyday the temple must have been visible many miles out to sea. It dates from the late Bronze Age but the Romans also added to it. The ancient kings of Paphos, some of whose gloomy tombs we entered, were also high priests of the temple of Aphrodite. They lived in great style, which was carried on by the kings of Neo-Paphos. Legend has it that one of these kept himself cool at mealtimes by using doves that hovered above his head but were prevented from landing by the king's attendants. What attracted the doves was oil made from fruit, which the king smeared on his head – which was, one hopes, bald.

JANUARY

Dearest Ma,

Tim's cousins chose to arrive on New Year's Eve, at midnight, and at Paphos airport on the other side of the island. Tim therefore missed the celebrations at Anna's hotel.

We were thankful our guests allowed only one week for their break from the English winter. Very soon it became apparent that they were not culture vultures, turning down offers to visit ruins, museums or monasteries. Up to the high Troodos we took them to visit the lovely villages of Platres and Prodhromos, the latter where portly King Farouk of Egypt, before his downfall, once had a summer villa. These villages, with their ghosts of the heady days of British rule, when the rich spent their summers here in expensive hotels, now cater for more run-of-the-mill types. The once famous Berengaria Hotel, the highest in Cyprus, is now in ruins. We lunched at the Hotel Splendid in Platres and then pressed on, it being very chilly indeed, with a light drift of snow on the pine forests. Most of the week was spent near or on the coast, our visitors being anxious for some sun and warmth, though we did bob in to view the Neolithic village of Khirokitia (7,000–3,000 BC) on the way. Around Aphrodite's birthplace, the great rock of Petra Tou Romiou, bathers sport themselves in summer. Here we walked our guests along its pebbly shore and the sun shone for us, a little weak but welcome.

The husband's only comment was that 'it is a pity that the island has no decent rivers'. His wife remarked on how cold the tiles were on their bedroom floor, but failed to notice the stunning view from the balcony, for Thekla has a holiday flat above her restaurant and that is where we had installed them. If our English visitor did notice the view she

166

was careful not to say so. The highlight of her visit seems to have been the ordering and purchasing of a black leather suit from a Limassol tailor. We found them both a deeply uninteresting couple and heaved a happy sigh at their departure.

Their two boys, aged ten and twelve, left little appreciative notes about the house and were altogether far more amenable. 'Tomorrow we have to go back to boring old England,' wrote Anthony sorrowfully. 'I hope you have a VERY good New Year in Cyprus, which I like a lot.' As we bade them goodbye we were glad to note that the pasty faces with which they had first greeted us were now glowing with rosy health. Anthony wears a Manchester United scarf, while Robert sports a Liverpool woolly hat. Poor things, going back to all that dank, dark weather!

O! The bliss at speeding some of our departing guests and the sorrow at the departure of others! Edmund, with his easy enjoyment of life, to say nothing of his bag of tools, will be forever welcome. I will continue this letter after Epiphany as we intend to go down to the coast to watch the procession.

All love,

L

Wednesday

The departure of Tim's tiresome cousins was the harbinger of several mighty storms this week, which rolled over the mountains and crashed down the valleys as though making sure the visitors had well and truly left. Each day I peer down the valley at our dam but it is difficult to tell whether the rains have made any real difference.

Together with the storms, Tim's spirits have done a nose dive. I suspect that the directors of the company which is largely responsible for financing the Law Conference are proving to be tricky. This can also be said of the female administrator who so irritates Tim. This is his first taste of dealing with the business world and the 'fat cats' who run it.

At the start of our sojourn here we were invited to a jolly evening at a Limassol restaurant, where Tim made a considerable hit by throwing himself into some Greek dancing with more enthusiasm than flair. He clasped one of the directors' wives by her portly waist and swept her on to the floor. However, he was not prepared for Greek dancing, where the men and women dance separately, and this threw him momentarily. However, he recovered his sang foid, though his long legs tended to trip up not just himself, but the other braves in the line. A burst of applause finished the performance, the loudest coming from our table. It was a good start but we have not been invited out again!

We are to receive a percentage of the profits from the Conference, so Tim is worried. As he does not wish to discuss his problems with me, I suggested he find a counsellor, but the idea went down like a lead balloon. He sets off for work cheerful enough, but the end of the day finds him cross and silent. The jaunty angle of his brown fedora and his new flannel suit, hand-tailored by Photis Photiades 'The Merchant Tailor', belies an angry spirit within. His appetite gets poorer every day, so that the smart suit begins to sag on its lanky frame. Each evening, as I hear his Jermyn Street shoes clonking on our stone laneway as he approaches home, I pray for a renaissance in our fortunes. He hides his worries from the village people, who greet him with cheerful shouts. 'Teem! Hello Teem! The Rover, she going OK? I find a good place for you to get new tyre. Very cheap. We go tomorrow, OK?' Or 'Teem, you come coffee house?'

Is Tim experiencing the Greek handshake?

6th January – Epiphany

This festival, to commemorate the visit of the wise men to

Bethlehem, is celebrated by casting a cross upon the waters. We drove down to Larnaca to watch. The procession set off from the ancient Byzantine church of Ayios Lazarus. A stone sarcophagus bearing the name of Lazarus was found hereabouts in AD 890 and a multi-domed church was erected above the tomb. After he was raised from the dead, Lazarus is said to have travelled from the Holy Land to Cyprus, where he was ordained as a bishop by St Barnabas. It is claimed he held this office for thirty years!

The procession moved at a slow pace along the town waterfront. Rather incongruously, it was led by a troupe of beefy-legged girls in blue berets and khaki skirts. Each girl clasped before her a stem of three white lilies. A cross made of white flowers, trailing long silver ribbons, was borne aloft behind them, and after the marching band came the clerics. In black robes and black toques, they were a sombre foil to the Archbishop, a splendid figure in golden robes and a glittering golden crown, somewhat reminiscent in shape to that worn by the Pharaohs of Lower Egypt (or was it Upper?). The pungent aroma of incense mingled with the fresh sea air. With his silver cross the Archbishop blessed the crowd. As the procession turned into the marina, we lost it in a rush of onlookers as everyone jockeyed for a position, but we managed to find a few precarious footholds on the rocks that shore up the harbour wall. The service was conducted through loud speakers, interrupted by two pleasure boats that began sounding their sirens at inopportune moments. A flock of white doves was released and circled the crowd, one alighting on the head of a spectator. A small replica of the cross was tossed into the waters and several young men, stripped to the waist, promptly dived into the sea to retrieve it.

Five years ago today Tim and I watched this very ceremony of Epiphany on the far shores of Western Australia. Under a midsummer sun marched the Greek community of Perth, the priests in their long black robes, the elderly ladies in black and the crowd following the silver cross down to the sparkling sea.

Back in the village, we found Evagora starting to cook a batch of *lokmades*, it being the custom at Ephiphany to hurl the first one out of the pan on to the roof to ward off evil spirits. Her boys were too hungry to waste even one, however, and scoffed the lot.

Tuesday

Coffee with Thekla this morning. We sit in her kitchen while little Thekla sleeps in her cot in a corner. The child's mother, the beautiful Stella, is in her lace shop in the village. Grandmother Thekla is not so busy now and we can sit and chat for half an hour. All is peace and serenity. The home-made sausages are in the fridge, having been disgorged from Thekla's 'mincing machine' like the entrails of some nameless beast. Thekla and Tassos beamed with amusement at my obvious distaste as the fat glutenous things emerged from their torture chamber. We sip our coffee now and my eyes stray to a plate next to a loaf of bread. The bodies of six tiny birds rest on it! Their eyes are closed, their wings folded. Thekla laughs at my look of horror.

'They are very good meat. Very sweet. They cost me one pound each,' she explains.

'But Thekla, these are beautiful wild birds!'

'Yes, they do not stay long in Cyprus. They are called *ambelopoulia*. They sing nicely. They are coming from somewhere.'

'Doesn't the government protect them?'

'Not these ones. They are very healthy. The meat is not polluted. They are very pure!' Thekla insists.

We both gaze at the six little bodies arranged in a heap. So small are they that they fit snugly on to a bread and butter plate. Three have black heads and soft, grey-green bodies. Three have reddish-brown caps. Perhaps they are three pairs of husbands and wives, wintering in our warmer climes?

'If I do not buy them someone else will,' Thekla shrugs. My dismay amuses her. We change the subject and inspect the lace

170

work which she somehow finds time to do on winter evenings. While Tassos and the boys watch television, Thekla pulls down her lamp and sews.

Sunday

I am no longer in good odour with Father S. At church this morning I committed a serious ecclesiastical faux pas. At the end of the service it is customary for the congregation to queue to receive the sacramental bread. The village people supply the loaves themselves and receive back a goodly supply, cut in thick chunks, to take home. I have never joined this queue but today something prompted me to do so. I awaited my turn behind Myrafora. When the moment came I received one piece of bread only and a penetrating look from the priest. As I reached the door a sharp voice called me back. Pointing an accusing finger Father S barked, 'You orthodox?'

I shook my head, guilty as a schoolgirl. Quick as a flash the bread was taken back! I retreated, catching as I did so an enigmatic smile from the cleric's wife as she cleared away the candles from the sconce.

The incident has left me chastened. I feel excluded. Cast out! This village, this place, does not belong to me any more. And yet, I was beginning to feel that it did.

Saturday

Today, 30th January, is the feast day of St Gregory, St John and St Basil.

This afternoon I found a mound of cut wood outside our front door that was blocking the lane. As I had not paid for it and the wood was in the way, I telephoned our woodman's wife, who works at the Co-op bank in the upper village. She replied that her husband would call by at some stage. Towards evening the doorbell rang and our 'charcoal burner', a rangy young man, dark-eyed and mien as handsome as a Romany's, was back. Unperturbed by the fact that he had given himself twice as much work as necessary, he began picking up the logs in his brawny arms and re-stacking them in our courtyard. A disused concrete flower bed beneath the eaves (installed by 'the other lady' tenant) serves as a useful area for a wood pile. I took pity on the poor fellow and added a bottle of wine for the extra effort he was making. He took it with a nonchalant grace but with a look that said he could as easily have done without it. This man, who chops his wood and burns his charcoal up on the quiet mountain, would not call the Queen his aunt.

This evening a scattering of snowflakes drifted down into the courtyard, settling on the bougainvillaea, which is still partly in bloom. It will soon get a severe haircut, its abundance of growth, fed by the sewer, having got a little out of hand. As fast as the bright petals fall, new ones burst forth, while the vigour of its growth makes a leafy archway over the courtyard steps and for most of the year sends cascades of colour along the verandahs, up over the walls and into the lane, much to the irritation of Evagora.

Our wood-burning stove in the parlour is a great success, provided the wind is in the right direction. We only get smoked out when it isn't. So, up to a point, Thekla was right. The missing pane of glass is still missing, but in our snug parlour we can look out at the gentle falling of the snow.

FEBRUARY

Friday

The weather was warm enough today, when the sun came out, for Anastasia and me to put our chairs outside her shop and hang some mats and tablecloths on her 'washing lines'. She has a small shop in one of the upper village's little side lanes. Some of the cloths we pinned on the wooden doors of a deserted house next door. The house has a deep courtyard viewed through imposing wrought iron gates and is filled with orange and lemon trees and a giant fig. Its ghostly balconies hang down in places where the supports are giving way, where the iron has rusted through. Once it was a splendid house. Who cares for it now?

Anastasia's shop is an arbour of lace. Even the ceiling is draped with it. Apart from the old Venetian designs worked on linen, there is intricate crochet work and 'Tuscany' lace. The latter has the delicacy of a spider's web. There are few elderly ladies left with such skills. Anastasia talked as she stitched.

'My mother was very strict with us. She made our lives a bit of a misery, really. We girls worked at the lace from the age of six. We were not allowed to go and play until she was satisfied we had done our work. The boys, my brothers, they did better, of course.

'My mother's life was very hard. My father was a carpenter. He made doors and shutters. My parents had no time to relax. It was work all the time and then bed, nothing in between. My mother, she did the work on the land as well as the house and the lace. She harvested the grapes and the olives and the carobs. The carobs were easier to harvest. You could knock them down with long sticks. We helped her, for if she employed too many people she made no profit. She brought them on the donkey to the market here.'

'Did you own your donkey?'

'No, we hired it.'

'And what about your home?'

'We had no electricity or running water. We needed heating when we were sitting making the lace, so we had a small coal fire, a brazier. A merchant would come to the house and give my mother the orders. We had oil lamps and we fetched water from the public taps. We had a wood stove to cook on in winter and a clay oven out in the yard. You've seen our clay ovens? My mother heated the water for us to wash and we had a small bath made out of a half urn. If an urn for the wine or the olives breaks, it makes a useful bath. There was a small hole to drain out the water.'

I recalled that I had seen a similar one to that described by Anastasia at the ancient city of Kourion, a second century BC bath made from a giant urn! Old customs die hard?

'Outside we washed the dishes,' Anastasia continued. 'We didn't have washing powders or detergents, of course, so we used bran, like the bran you give the chickens, made into a mash. There were chickens, in the house, you know.' Anastasia gave a self-conscious laugh. 'They were in small coops. You could make the dishes sparkle when you rubbed them with the bran. Everything was very healthy then. Nothing artificial. People lived to a good age. My mother was eighty-five when she died. She was very small, though. Only five feet high. My grandmother was even smaller. I myself am five feet four inches.'

'What did you eat?'

'We did not eat much meat. That was healthy. We could not afford much but we ate it on Sundays and on Thursdays. Then we fasted, forty days before Christmas and forty days before Easter. No animal products were allowed, so we became vegans. And of course from the first of August until the fourteenth we fasted. That was for the birth of the Virgin Mary. You can imagine what a feast we had when Christmas came. We were so glad.

'This little street here, it was full of life! But about twenty years ago people just packed up and left. There was a blacksmith, a candle maker (he made the headpieces for the bridal veils, the ones with the little wax flowers on them). Then there was a shoemaker and a butcher, and a baker was on the corner over there. There were so many different smells when you went past. There was so much life! The women would have to get up from their chairs to let a donkey go by. There was so much talk and chatter!'

Dearest Ma,

It's really disgraceful that after all these years the Greek and Turkish powers that be cannot or will not settle the 'Cyprus problem'. Last year a small concession was reached in allowing Greek and Turkish Cypriots to visit a chosen church or a mosque in the two divided areas, though we are told that in Northern Cyprus life is much more secular than here in the south.

Over twelve hundred Turkish Cypriots, therefore, visited the Hala Sultan Tekke mosque in Larnaca to mark the end of the holy month of Ramadan. The mosque, the third holiest Islamic shrine after Mecca and Medina, was built in memory of the Prophet Mohammed's aunt, Umm Hasam, who is said to have died on this spot after falling from her mule. The recent deputation of pilgrims made up the largest number to cross the border since the Turkish invasion of the island in 1974. They were charged two pounds a head for the visas.

However, Rauf Denktash, the Turkish Cypriot leader, has imposed a fifteen pound visa fee on all Greek Cypriot pilgrims crossing to the north, together with a hefty charge for all those wishing to make special journeys to designated churches. Some of these churches have been looted, their valuable icons stolen and sold abroad, and a well-known fifteenth-century monastery is to become a tourist hotel with a casino!

A thousand Greek Cypriot pilgrims, intending to cross the border next Easter to visit the monastery of Apostolos Andreas on the Karpass Peninsula, have cancelled their Easter Pilgrimage. *The Cyprus Weekly,* which keeps us up to date with events, reports that Mr Denktash's visa payments have become too high.

On a more cheerful note, spring flowers are appearing all over the hills and by the roadside verges. The broom is already out and the delicate yellows of the charlock and flag lilies harmonize with the mauve of the wild orchids and the dog violets. The pomegranates in the garden of the deserted house opposite are just turning a little red where the early sun catches them.

All love

Libby

Sunday

I cannot persuade Tim to go back to his painting. Surely such good therapy! His watercolours and brushes lie unused in a drawer. His pen and ink washes of London scenes are the glory of the enchanting little guide to London which he published when still in his early twenties. There is so much to paint here, so many quaint old churches of varying architectural styles, starting with our five chapels and our Ayios Maria, a graceful white stone building with an imposing tapered tower. I know that Katerina is having a detrimental effect on Tim's equilibrium. This makes him less and less communicative, and more inclined to smoke more than he should.

Monday

Deep snow on Mount Olympus today, but the winter falls have been patchy. The Cypriots call the mountain Chionistra, which refers to the snow that falls there rather than to the home of the Greek gods. There are three ski lifts and a ski school up there but Tim and I, not being of a hearty build, have not ventured forth on to the slopes. His legs would get in the way.

A rare snowfall has blanketed Athens and Jerusalem. Winter has brought lashing winds as well as hail, knocking the delicate almond blossoms off the trees below our village. Any rain is welcomed by the villagers, but the Water Development Department is in gloomy mood and has announced that the winter rains have done little to ease the critically low levels in the dams. Peering down our valley from the roof terrace, we can see no water level at all in our dam. I continue with my frugal shower at night while Tim has his one and a half inches of bath water reminiscent of the wartime advice of King George VI. Being English, he will not take a shower. World Water Day is next week. There is a prophecy that the next conflict in the Eastern Mediterranean will be over water rather than borders.

In Nicosia yesterday we felt a surge of guilt at taking the Mazda to a car wash. Its white bodywork had all but vanished beneath a coating of reddish brown dust from a nasty khamasin wind blowing in from Egypt recently. The sandstorm closed airports and harbours from southern Egypt to the Lebanon and Greece. Cyprus all but vanished under a thick brownish haze. One of the grounded planes at Larnaca airport had the British Foreign Secretary, Robin Cook, on board, en route, he hoped, for Egypt.

MARCH

Wednesday

I have decided to rent, or rather sub-rent, an empty shop in the village. At the moment Thekla is the tenant but she has offered it to me for £30 a month. A business woman to her fingertips, she will not come down a single cent. Compared to the rent she is charging us for a whole house, this new rent seems much out of proportion, the shop consisting of one room only, with ill-fitting glass doors beneath which the village dust blows in relentlessly. I will use it as a studio.

There is a local campaign, backed by Greenpeace, to stop British military exercises taking place in the unspoilt region of the Akamas. These exercises are due to begin in a week. The Union of Democratic Youth of Paphos and The Committee Against British Policy and the Bases in Cyprus have called on the Cyprus government to help protect this region and 'the wishes of the Cyprus people'.

Here, since pre-history, the green and the loggerhead turtles have made their nests. Contemporaries of the dinosaurs, these stoic creatures have existed for over 150 million years. The glare from car and restaurant lights near beaches now disorientates the female turtles, who navigate hundreds of miles back to the same breeding grounds each year.

In Cyprus, turtles and their eggs have been legally protected since 1971 and in 1978 the Fisheries Department launched a unique project by founding a turtle hatchery in the Akamas. Nests are often collected from 'dangerous' beaches and transferred to the hatchery, where they are re-buried and protected by wire cages. Staff at the hatchery monitor the nest and ensure that the newly hatched turtles reach the sea in safety. There is a very high success rate and every year over six thousand baby turtles reach the sea. However, out of this number only about one in a hundred will reach full maturity. A few years ago a loggerhead turtle with severe head injuries was given a life-saving operation by a Nicosia neurosurgeon and was successfully returned to the sea.

Upon enquiring whether we could visit the hatchery to view this annual miracle, we were informed it means a pre-dawn, or rather after-midnight, start. We are pondering the idea.

25th March (Day of the Annunciation, an important day in the Church calendar)

'Silver' Chris is making an embossed silver lamp for the new church of the Prophet Elijah, (the little white one on top of the hill). The sun having come out again, he is working away at it under the mulberry tree by the car park. He may catch a stray, out-of-season tourist if he is lucky and thus steer them towards his little shop. He will put three silver angels on the lamp and a chain so that it can hang before the icon of the Virgin. Chris's English is self-taught, partly through his own efforts and partly through the help of his English-born Cypriot wife. They have three young children, one of whom rattles with relentless monotony past my shop studio in his plastic motorcar, while the other two do their best to distract my efforts with faces pressed to the glass doors.

Today is also Greek Independence Day and a public holiday.

APRIL

Wednesday

'Careful, Walter! Mind the drainpipe – go forwards! No, no. I mean go *back* a little. Oh dear.'

It was before 6 a.m. and the urgency of the woman's voice sent us leaping from bed. Looking down, we saw, to our utter amazement, a large white saloon car wedged into the right angle where our two lanes meet. With not so much as an inch to separate it from the high stone walls that held it prisoner, it was a wondrous sight.

The owner of the anxious voice was a smartly dressed woman in a bright red suit and high heels, with an immaculately coiffed head.

Evagora, in slippers and apron, had come out also.

'People don't normally come along here,' she was telling the couple. 'Well, not in cars, I mean.'

'No, that's what I told Walter. I said to him, "You've just gone through the No Entry sign".'

Walter, at the wheel, said nothing.

Dragging on a shirt and some trousers, Tim hurried downstairs. I got dressed and followed, just in time to hear the wife telling Evagora that they were 'following the diversion to the airport'.

'Diversion to the airport?' Evagora gasped. 'But we are in the mountains!'

Just as she spoke, there was a sickening crunch as Walter, revving hard, let go the clutch.

By now Andreas had appeared with Marcos and Andreas' beefy brother-in-law from the house opposite. Tim suggested that Walter get out while he and the three men just arrived put their shoulders to the wheel, so to speak.

As there was barely room for shoulders let alone the rest of them, the feat of 'jumping' the vehicle into a better position was tried. This was abandoned. At length, by a process of heaving the thing inch by inch, they got the car straight enough to be driven either forwards or back by minute degrees. Once satisfied that the situation looked more hopeful, Tim got into the driving seat. Walter, whose complexion had gone a deep bluish-red, stood by, breathing heavily. His wife kept her distance, taking a powder case out of her Gucci handbag and dabbing at her face.

'Isn't your husband a good driver?' she commented unfeelingly. We stood and watched as Tim reversed the vehicle up the lane within a hair's breadth of all our pretty pots. Behind trudged poor Walter, blowing hard, his gammy knee adding to his misery.

'What time do you have to be at the airport?' someone asked. It was now around 7.30 a.m.

'Departure time is eight,' the wife replied tartly. When the pair were safely installed in their car again, Tim got into his Rover and guided them on to the Larnaca road. It was a kindly gesture but, from the point of catching a plane, sadly futile.

Evagora wiped tears of laughter away with her apron.

'A diversion! Poor things!'

Thursday

It is wonderful to have our swallows back but there was a great rumpus in the courtyard early this morning. Frantic chatterings in the eaves set off the parrots, whose louder voices woke us at dawn. Two tiny eggs lie smashed on the courtyard floor. For some time we have wondered why *three* swallows are building this one nest. Is the maiden aunt back? Surely three is a crowd? This is how it now appears to be. Too many cooks have spoiled the broth. A squabble has ended in a small tragedy.

Easter Saturday

A hot day heralding the true start of summer. We met Nicos by the disused olive press on the other side of the village.

'Eleven a.m. sharp!' he had said. 'Elias is coming up here especially and you mustn't waste his time.'

'Of course not,' we agreed. 'But isn't he retired?'

'He's doing the chanting. It being Easter and all that. Didn't you know he does the chanting? You two! I dunno.'

Nicos' scorn when he discovers yet more of our ignorance of village matters is never spared us. Having caught us out again, he led us down the dusty road with an authoritative air. Just beyond an orange grove we halted. The air was heady with the scent of blossom, the oranges hanging like myriads of bright lanterns among the dark green leaves. Beneath the trees the ground buzzed with happy bees having a field day among the yellow daisies.

'This is it,' Nicos announced. As yet, there was no sign of the owner. 'You'll get your three bedroom house in here. No problem. And you can put your garage *here*.' He waved expansively. 'See this road? This is all going to be tarmacked for you.'

'Oh no!' we said in unison. 'That would be *awful*.'

'Do we know the actual size of the plot?' Tim asked as Nicos moved off, pacing his way through the tall grass with gusto.

'The border goes over there to that tree,' Nicos shouted, 'and comes along down past here to that carob, across to that other carob and then back along the road here, give or take. You'll have plenty of room.'

Nicos' assumption that, but for a few minor details, the land was already ours, was catching.

'Don't get me wrong, you two. If you don't want a tarmac road you needn't have it. Jesus Christ! You foreigners with your arty ideas! The tarmac can come up to here. No further, if that's what you want.'

We began to pace about 'our' land. Tim made off in one direction, I in another. We dodged about among lemon trees

182

burdened with fruit the size of tennis balls. The bees were too busy to notice us. At last there was a friendly shout on the still air. A stocky figure appeared on the would-be-tarmacadamed road. Elias shook hands. He produced a measuring tape and he and Nicos, taking one end each, wobbled it along to the giant carob in one corner and then, dodging clumps of fennel with a not too fussy attention to accuracy, took it down to a spot just short of the orange grove. Some minutes later, Nicos returned.

'You see that stone wall, there? Well, you can knock it down.'

'But it's a beautiful wall!'

'Look.' Nicos did his best to keep his patience. 'Do you want this extra bit of land or don't you? If you knock the wall down you'll get the bit you lose over there.'

'But the wall is holding up that neighbour's terrace! And what do you mean by "*lose*" exactly?'

Nicos, temporarily cornered, tried another tack. 'See this tree, Liz?'

'Yes.'

'Well, it's protected, but you didn't know that? Protected by the government! It can't be chopped down.' He leant heavily against it to make his point. 'Being on the edge of your land here, beside the road, like, it means you won't get lorries down this way. Be too narrow for 'em. So really, you're gaining. The land you've lost down that end there' – he gestured vaguely – 'won't matter. You've got it here.'

It was simpler to agree, to pretend that we didn't mind the fact that our land now appeared to be triangular instead of rectangular, or that the disadvantages of having no space available for a garage – or come to that, a garden – were far outweighed by the possession of a removable wall and a government-protected tree.

'Well, thanks, Nicos. Thanks very much for your help. We'll have to consider all this, of course. The price and everything. Could you explain this to Elias?'

The landlord wasn't listening. His attention had been caught by mole-like workings at the other end of his plot. These had

184

been left by local villagers in their search for the root of the lisari plant. These roots provide the dye for the Easter eggs. Tim and I are doing our best to work our way through a batch, but there is a limit to the number of hard-boiled eggs one can digest at any given time, and magenta coloured ones at that. No sooner is one offering finished off than another arrives on our doorstep.

Elias appeared unruffled by the fact that a sizeable chunk of his plot had been turned into a mini earth-moving works. He smiled cheerfully as we all shook hands and departed, we two homewards, Nicos to the coffee house and our landlord back to his chanting. We got the impression that whether or not he sold us his land was not one of his major concerns.

Monday

What to do with two more grandsons in April? A friend had mentioned camels so off we went to find some. In the old days, camels and camel trains were a familiar sight on the island, some carrying loads of salt from the great salt lake near Larnaca. Now, the salt has become polluted and only the pink rash of flamingoes, which fly in to catch the seasonal shrimp, make use of this once profitable area.

We found our camels, several dozen of them, the males of uncertain temper being segregated in their own yards. One, a feisty beast, was roaring away in a decidedly testy manner but the owner explained that camels are really very agreeable, if treated kindly. A camel ride on a Queensland beach is one of the distinctive memories of my childhood. There you are, perched as high as an eagle in its eyrie but first of all are the preliminaries to getting there. You mount your animal while he is seated and then, without warning, you are tipped forwards, almost from your saddle, as the beast gets his back legs uncurled. Then there is the corresponding lurch backwards as his front legs manoeuvre themselves into the vertical position (or is it the other way round?).

185

However, James and Timmy missed out on this essential experience as the camel man hoisted each child aloft, one camel each, and set off. James wanted another go after that. Timmy did not.

The rest of the week was swimming in a most luxurious indoor pool at one of Limassol's expensive hotels. At least these two boys saw more of the island than did their scuba-diving brothers last year.

Tuesday

My attempts this week to get on with my painting – a landscape – have been thwarted. No sooner do I get started than half a dozen faces appear at the studio's glass doors, small noses pressed flat against the panes. Should I ignore them, a hammering starts, this rising in a crescendo as more children join in, two of the girls as boisterous as their brothers. The weather having grown exceedingly hot, I long to open these doors but must instead gasp my way through the morning with the room hermetically sealed. I have promised several parents that their children may come, four at a time, to the house for some art work should they so wish. However, this treat will only happen if they leave me alone while I am doing mine.

Dearest Ma,

Old Crystalla (our neighbour) returned home for Easter. Her frail form has grown smaller still so that the tall pew she occupies in church seems to all but envelop her, while her thick spectacles grow larger.

Olive branches and bay leaves, oil and bread – these components are used by these Mediterranean people to celebrate Easter. On Good Friday the people bring bay leaves, which the priest blesses and scatters over them as well as all over the floor of the church. At home, they prepare their own offerings of bay leaves which, held in small clay goblets and then lit, emit a gentle fragrance. Olive branches are brought to the church on Palm Sunday.

At 11 p.m. on Easter Saturday night, the church was packed to capacity. However, there were plenty of young men and boys whose duty it was to see to the bonfire. Soon loud explosions and merry shouts were rending the air in tandem with the service; the church doors were shut to moderate some of this noise. The weather being exceedingly hot and the building crowded to the last squeeze, we sat in a sauna-like atmosphere as the lengthy proceedings progressed. At last the lights were switched off, the flames from the bonfire making dancing patterns of light on the dim icons and the faces of the waiting congregation. Some of these were unfamiliar to us, those who once lived here but were now scattered; some, having prospered, were now enjoying a lifestyle very different from that of their parents. Some were smartly dressed, the men in suits, the women in the latest fashions. A few young girls dared to wear the forbidden trousers or jeans, or here and there, mini skirts. The elderly were dressed, as always: the women in their black headscarves revealing glimpses of faces worn patient by time. Then Father S appeared through a door in the iconostasis. He held a tall lighted candle whose flame was passed about the congregation until each of us had lit our candle, one from the other. Low murmurs of 'Christos anesti! Alithinos anesti' (Christ is risen! He is truly risen!) passed from row to row as the Easter event was greeted with smiles and nods and a sudden draught of fresh air as the doors were flung open once more.

Emerging from the church at midnight, we were greeted by the bonfire roaring away, dangerously close, and the fireworks whizzing and spitting. Father S, looking weary in his heavy and many-layered vestments, reprimanded a youth for noisy behaviour. Tomorrow, perhaps, our priest can have a day off and go tend his fruit trees. For a moment, one of the fireworks, an iridescent, fizzing arrow, appeared to be heading for a collision with the rising moon. Just short of its target it exploded into a myriad tiny fireballs and the moon sailed onwards, unmolested. Should we leave the island, I will truly miss the Greek Orthodox way of commemorating Easter. Here secularization has been kept at bay, but for how long? I envy the deep piety of these people, particularly the old people. I sit and watch them in church, the old women in their black garb. How I wish I was Rembrandt and could do justice to those calm, careworn faces!

On Easter Sunday families sport their new clothes and go on picnics, taking grilled *souvla* (skewered lamb) and hard-boiled eggs dyed a purplish-red!

All love,

Libby

Friday

This is the fourth time during the last fortnight that I have had to telephone Philippos reminding him that we need another calor gas refill. Philippos is a cheerful lad with apple-red cheeks and a broad grin. I am not sure whether the grin is perpetual or whether he keeps it in readiness for my appalling Greek. Up till now, the telephone conversation has gone like this:

Me: *Kalimera Philippos! Pos iste? Hrizome gaz, simera, parakalo. Thekla spiti. Sas efkaristo. Adio.*
Philippos (or his mother or grandmother): *Thekla spiti? OK.*

Roughly translated and very literally: Good morning, Philippos! How are you? I want gas, today, please. Thekla's house. Many thanks. Goodbye.

Although the system has worked relatively well to date, this last fortnight it has broken down completely. After placing my order, I leave the requisite two pounds thirty-five cents in an envelope tucked into the top of the empty canister on our front doorstep. Sometimes the envelope is there for some days before Philippos appears in his dilapidated truck. This time it stayed there for nearly a week and then vanished. I discussed this disappearance with Evagora.

'It must have been those Russian tourists,' she said. 'I never do trust them!'

'You could be right,' I said doubtfully. 'Though its never happened before.'

'They're bringing all these drugs into the island, these Russians! And the women are running off with our men! We had those tourists come through the village yesterday when you were out. Yes, it's very probably them.'

However, Evagora was wrong. It turns out that Androulla, down the lane, had taken it into her own hands to sort out my problem. She had replaced the empty canister with a new one of her own, collected the envelope and gone home, satisfied with her neighbourly act. The only flaw in all this was that she had forgotten to mention the matter. Evagora, having decided on some detective work, gave poor Androulla such a pasting for her trouble that I hurried outdoors to find out what the row was about. The two women were at it hammer and tongs. Evagora's rapid torrents vied in speed and shrillness with Androulla's. For a moment it seemed the two women might come to blows. I slunk back indoors. After some five to ten minutes the pair of them entered my kitchen, all smiles again. Evagora agreed to thank Androulla for her trouble on my behalf and to congratulate her on her herculean efforts in having dragged a heavy canister some three hundred yards homewards and then an even heavier one back. Neither women, of course, thought this remarkable.

'The women of Cyprus. They are the Amazons,' says artist Maria.

189

Today I asked Evagora if she knew what had happened to Philippos.

His grandfather has died. Had I not seen the funeral passing by?

Tuesday

Australians seem happier to sample our home comforts than do the English. Sue and Leycester Meares of Sydney arrived last week and squashed themselves into our spare room with great humour. Leycester's tall, lanky form dwarfed Thekla's mother's wardrobe which, together with the bureau with the sticking drawers, takes up a good deal of vital space. We took them to the usual places of interest, Sue taking copious notes for her diary. In between times, Leycester took himself off for long walks, striding across the landscape in boots and shorts, indifferent to the rough terrain and the scratches that covered his hairy legs. Offering to cook us chops, his comments on our barbecue facilities do not bear repeating. While we make do with a tin dish and a scattering of coals, all balanced on the roof terrace wall, his Sydney counterpart is a good one and a half metres in length, has an impressive array of knobs and slides about on wheels.

Saturday

One of my most aesthetic pleasures is hanging out the washing. This, and sweeping up the bougainvillaea blossoms on the snow-white courtyard steps, are chores to be relished.

Our washing line is strung from one balcony to another. The sheets must be folded a bit in the nesting season in order not to disorientate the swallows. However, folded or not, they are bone dry in minutes. A dreamy contemplation of the hazy distances accompanies the placing of each peg: nothing to compare with

190

the frustrating efforts back in England. (Drape the jolly stuff over the indoor 'rack', bunch it up to get everything on, check it every day or so to test whether it is ready yet for the airing cupboard. No? Still damp? Then leave it for another day!) The sheets here come off the line as crisp as corn flakes and as sweet-smelling as a garden.

Monday

A minor altercation has been going on in the village. One of the silversmiths has, for some time, wished to extend his business by renting an empty shop that lies strategically placed to the car park. From here he could keep an eye out for the first visitors while pursuing some of his work, rain or shine. A shop with a roof is better than a spot under a mulberry tree. His work consists of hammering out sheets of silver over a template, a job that requires no more complicated apparatus than a small hammer and a table. The items thus produced are usually for the church, such as lamps and containers for incense. The shop that the silversmith has his eye on has, for some years, been rented by his aunt, who wishes to keep it empty to avoid extra competition for her daughter's shop, not quite so well placed. The owner of the shop lives abroad and as her visits are once a year, the participants must bide their time before a settlement is reached. There is a whiff of tension in the air.

Friday

An unseasonal May thunderstorm today has disconcerted our swallows. Torrential rain has curbed their sorties from their nest and the anxious parents hang about, deprived of roving insects while trying to quieten the babies. These have become distinctly noisier over the past twenty-four hours, their voices more like

feeble squeaks than hoarse raspings. The parents poke at the nest, administering imaginary food into cavernous mouths, and then mother swallow settles down to warm the brood while father goes off between downpours. The swallows' discomfort has curbed some of the pleasure of seeing the rain.

Meanwhile Pyramus and Thisbe are equally preoccupied down below. During the nest-building business, Thisbe was particularly busy. Carefully 'chewing' off thin slivers of wood from the branches we have placed in the aviary, she tucks one piece at a time under her wing. She then flies back to her nest box, 'comin' in on a wing and a prayer', so to speak. The plastic roof sheeting that Edmund made now has a scalloped edge to it where both husband and wife have chewed bits off for use as a nest liner. Now Pyramus sits on his perch like a disconcerted grass widower. His time will come later. Thisbe is inside most of the day. So far she has laid two eggs.

The widowed Pinky devotes herself these days to a leisurely life, comforted by her children. Her remaining son, Claudius, whom the rat failed to eat, has taken up residence in her nestbox and the pair seem content.

MAY

Monday

Today *The Cyprus Weekly* reports that the government has lodged another protest with the UN Headquarters in New York over the destruction of Greek Orthodox churches in the occupied areas of northern Cyprus. Turkish reports announce that more than one hundred Orthodox churches have been turned into mosques or cafés or stables since the 1974 invasion. In our part of the island the mosques in the towns and villages are looked after by caretakers and, although closed, are kept clean and tidy. We can see from our terrace the minaret of the little mosque in the upper village close to Maria's house. These people, the Greek and Turkish Cypriots, managed to live together in relative harmony for centuries. True, there were some disturbances. But had the politicians not meddled, the old days that many Greek Cypriots tell us they miss, could be back.

Thursday

A funeral procession this morning passed the little general store halfway up the hill. The little, elderly priest from the upper village, with grey flowing beard, walked in front, swinging the incense. The bier followed, mounted on a small open truck bedecked with black drapes and swatches of golden material. Festoons of black feathers adorned the four corners of the supporting frame. The mourners, about a dozen in number, walked behind. The boxes of bright red tomatoes and capsicums that front the store, the lesser red and orange of apples and carrots, the bright green cucumbers and paler green of the wilting lettuces and parsley, the purple aubergines, all were a foil to the black and sombre little procession that wound past like figures in a pageant, shoes grey with dust. The procession moved down the hill, the tinkling bells growing fainter as did the heady smell of incense.

A passing of a life amongst such abundance of life.

JUNE

Sunday

Midsummer Day has come and gone. One or two of our swallows still roost in the courtyard but the others have left. Sometimes they all come back, swooping and circling under the eaves to check on their old birthplace. The cicadas hum loudly in the still hot air. Old Demetri does not seem to be feeding his cat. She is mewing up and down the lane but turns her nose up at some cold sausage we offer her.

This evening we have drinks with George and Zoe up in their 'castle' overlooking the upper village. We sit on the terrace and have a grandstand view towards Nicosia to the north, glimmering ahead in the hazy distance, and then to the right, down towards the sea. The mountains turn pinkish in the evening light. Zoe's roses are doing well in spite of the winds they get up here, and her white jasmine scents the air. Her small son, Marios, picks a sprig and presents it to me with a courtly grace.

I notice Tim accepting a second generous whisky from George, whose forty-eighth birthday it is. George's eldest son has just become engaged to a girl in Scotland but the young couple will live in Cyprus. George and Zoe are very pleased. Suddenly, George announces that he has a 'machine gun'.

'Yes,' says George. 'I have a gun.' He instructs the six-year-old Marios to go and fetch it. It is almost as big as the boy. It is an evil-looking thing but most definitely not a machine gun. Father and son play with it. Marios removes the cartridge holder with expert hands, beaming his pleasure.

'The Turks?' we ask, unnecessarily.

George nods. 'We must be ready. This has a range of many metres. It is good.'

In the distance deep mauve shadows fill the hollows in the hills. Everything is still.

Monday

My foray today into the bridge-playing, expatriate community will be my last.

A rather bossy woman calling herself Veronica left a message on our answering machine last week. Would I fill in for a missing player? Determined to decline, I telephoned back. Fortunately she was out, so I left my message. Veronica replied to my call. I do not play bridge, I told her, well, certainly not *her* kind. I play a chatty, family-type game and anyway, it must be twenty years... Veronica, however, persisted. She quite understood but, on the other hand, my failure to turn up would throw out one whole table and spoil everyone's day! Weakly, I agreed.

Determined not to disgrace myself, I arrived punctually at 9.30 but there was no sign of Veronica. We were holding our session in a taverna beside the sea on far too nice a day to be indoors. Someone led me to a table where two large matronly women awaited my arrival. There were curt introductions and with no time for me to explain that I was a *very* raw recruit, we started.

'Why did you lead *that*?'

The woman opposite me, my partner for the first few games, glared across the green baize in my direction, indignation mounting in her ample bosom.

'Give her a chance, Dorothy,' said the chap on my right. 'This game is only a warm-up, after all.'

Everyone knew how to score and kept little pads under their right elbows on to which they made busy calculations at the end of each chukka. I discovered we were playing the Chicago Convention (or was it Philadelphia?). Or was it something else? Soon I began sticking to my seat, perspiration dripping from me in rivulets. I was not sorry to leave Dorothy behind, the chap on my right having volunteered with unexpected chivalry to partner me. We did fairly well. I managed, somehow, not to trump any of his aces. After each round, my partner and I got up and moved to the next table, where the ordeal began again.

At lunchtime I sprang from my chair and walked out on to the beach, munching a sandwich. Most of the players looked as if they never left their tables, even to eat. In fact, some didn't but ate their feta salads and omelettes as though they were born, lived and died playing bridge, only to halt for meals and other vital functions. Several players gave me startled looks as though I was committing some dreadful faux pas for leaving without permission. A short excursion to the wc was allowed, however. Thirty minutes later my happy beachcombing was interrupted by anxious cries.

'Libby, we're starting! Hurry!'

'Do you know the Milwauke Convention?' someone asked. A deathly silence followed my reply, which was that I found it safer, really, to play by instinct. No danger, whatever, of being invited again.

Tuesday

Maria has lost her battle with the courts. She must now pay rent for the Turkish chicken coops in which she was rehoused by the Greek Cypriot government. This is a blow, as the transformation she has wrought on the two buildings should be rewarded, so much of her time and effort and money have gone into the work. She has built what we in Australia call a cathedral roof over her large airy studio, urging the builders on by doing some of the work herself. Both the studio and sitting room are large and airy with stone flagged floors, as is the long verandah that runs the length of the house front. So the two chicken coops are now one house. The Turkish Cypriots who once lived here, though in very reduced circumstances, had one of the best views from this village, views extending for miles down the broad valleys and over the hills. Maria is an expert at finding bargains in old shops or in turning bits of things she finds on her walks into useful pieces of furniture. The Cypriot's habit of untidy rubbish dumping can be a boon for such people. An old iron bedstead, draped with rugs, is perfect for outdoor siestas, and two doors with wire netting stretched between make an aviary outside her bedroom: Garden plants sprout from buckets, teapots, olive jars. Even roses grow here beside the twining jasmine, and in spring narcissi, daffodils and jonquils flourish between the stones. Her myriads of cats, however, discourage the birds. New York must seem a century ago, another planet. As for the home she and her family lost in Famagusta, no compensation has come from the Turks.

Wednesday

Anna is happy. The hotel no longer has water shortage problems. Her village is buying water from a private contractor. What is more, she has won a Gold Star Award for the hotel. These mountain villages have stiff competition from the attractions offered on the coast. By and large, the latter are sapping business away as more and more Northern European holiday-makers, desperate for warmth and sun, flock to the beaches. Ayia Napa, which we first visited in 1980, is now unrecognizable. On that

holiday I can remember how my daughter and I giggled in alarm as our taxi driver bumped us across mile after mile of dry, stony, desert-like country in search of our Shangri-La. Our hotel, which we reached at length, was nowhere near the sea, but perched on a dusty hillside with a patch of bright green lawn in front. On this, sprinklers played the precious water while we felt a little guilty, knowing how desperately it was needed by the farmers. A minibus bumped us down a narrow track for our daily sea-bathing. Will the Akamas, one of the last unspoilt areas in the south, survive? Ayia Napa nowadays is strictly for the young, but in the future will the gentle turtle who comes to lay her eggs in the Akamas beaches be allowed to return?

JULY

Saturday

A heatwave this week. It is forty degrees in Nicosia.

Evagora turned down our offer to take Michaelis swimming today. She is convinced he will drown. 'Oh no! It is too dangerous!'

We tried to explain that the water in our favourite little bay is shallow near the shore and that Michaelis could come to no harm. But she would have none of it. We doubt that any of her family has ever been near the sea. It is useless to try to persuade Evagora to come herself. Her duty to her family is paramount and she stands by her post come hell or high water. Today, this provides a good excuse. As for Michaelis, he will go kick a football about under a blazing sun.

We can think of nothing more delectable than a swimming lesson in all this heat and feel sorry about Michaelis. If I had had lessons here instead of in the fenced-in piece of sea in Southern Queensland, where bronzed and brawny Mrs Bell held her classes, my development as a swimmer might have been somewhat different. As it is, the sport leaves me floundering, but the sea here is delicious and shallow enough by the shore for the less adventurous.

Our swimming 'pool' in Queensland was fathoms deep and hedged about by wooden palings slippery with green slime and spiked with oysters and barnacles. A dive might bring you eyeball to eyeball with a jellyfish. Returning to the edge of the baths, your struggles to gain a handhold on one of the palings could well be thwarted by some haughty crab edging its tentative way across the barnacles, its stalk-like glare cold and suspicious. I have always disliked crabs, particularly since one of Dad's impoverished patients started sending them to us in lieu of payment. They arrived in a cardboard suitcase and made frightening scaping noises with their claws. Taken into the kitchen, the poor things were soon dispatched by Cook with the carving knife. 'You must always

202

do that,' my mother told her. 'It is cruel to throw them into boiling water.'

Down at the baths, 'Reach out! Reach out,' Mrs Bell would call, dragging as she did so a rag doll on a long rope just ahead of you. Unable to touch bottom, you reached out, frantically. Somehow the rag doll was never within your grasp.

No. Mrs B's swimming classes were no fun at all.

But Michaelis – does he know what he is missing?

Wednesday

The heatwave is still with us.

Last evening Tim and I heard a commotion outside and found Andreas holding up a small snake. He held it by its tail, having crushed its triangular-shaped head with a stone. It had an attractively patterned body. We were sorry he had killed it, for the thing was not poisonous, he said. However, he thought it was after our parrots. Our young guest mourned the death of Andreas' dead snake. She, a German woman, has been two or three times to stay at Anna's hotel. It would appear that for some years now she has been trying to extricate herself from an unsatisfactory relationship back home. While here, her determination to do so grows. However, in spite of a good deal of well-meant advice from Anna and the rest of us, and encouraging signals from our new friend that she will, on her return, grasp the nettle, she is soon back, the nettle still ungrasped.

Today, she came for lunch. 'It is very beautiful,' she said regretfully, bending down to stroke the snake's pulsating body.

This is the third snake that has been run to ground in our corner of the village this week. The hot weather is bringing them out in search of water. Marcos removed a black one, some four feet long, from outside the house several days ago. To our surprise he did not kill it, but grasping it by the head, carried it up to his truck to free it later. The Cypriot, so fond of killing wildlife, respects the good work done by these grass snakes.

203

Tim has blocked up the opening for our water duct in the courtyard wall. While doing this, he and I are aware that a snake can climb anything, if it chooses. We will have to put extra wire mesh on the aviary. Taking further precautions, I threw out the water in the birdbath on the roof. From here a snake may slither down on to the aviary roof with little difficulty, have a drink and do further mischief.

Saturday

I have just experienced the excellence of private health care on this island. To wit: my gall bladder was whipped out in a Nicosia clinic this week and two days later I am home. The kindly surgeon, whose praises I cannot sing highly enough, asked me if I wished proof of his efforts, in a small glass jar, but I thanked him and declined. Apparently he did not use keyhole surgery, but something akin to it, with the result that I felt nothing and have a minute piece of sticking plaster on my abdomen as the only evidence of his work.

SEPTEMBER

Saturday

Evagora and Andreas have a daughter! On returning from our two months' summer break in England, we stumbled yesterday past piles of builder's rubble in the lane – sacks of cement, a water tank, bricks and shovels. We edged our suitcases past, and moments later Evagora, all breathless excitement, was hurrying into our kitchen.

Angelo, their eldest son, has brought home a wife. We returned with Evagora to view the photograph standing proud on the dresser in the front parlour.

'She's beautiful!' we said. 'Really beautiful.'

The photograph showed a young woman with luxurious strands of blonde hair, blue eyes and the fine facial bones of a Slav.

'Yes,' Evagora agreed. 'She is lovely. She is from Russia. Well, the Ukraine really. They will marry soon.'

Gone is Evagora's prejudice against the dreaded Russians!

'Well, Evagora, now you've got your daughter. The daughter you always wanted!'

Andreas came in as we spoke. Grinning from ear to ear, he sank heavily into his armchair and began removing his boots. Unlike his wife, he speaks no English. Andreas was once a silversmith but his eyes became damaged through his work with a blow lamp and he resorted to farming a smallholding of sheep down by the dam. When he smiles he is really handsome, and now he is all smiles.

'And all that building work going on on your roof is for the happy couple?'

'Yes. It is small but it will do them for the moment. They will have just the bedroom and their own bathroom. Later they will have their own place.' The fact that the annexe has been built from breeze blocks and not the regulation local stone seems to have been overlooked by the powers that be.

The new 'daughter' is already at work in the upper village and learning to make the lace.

Tuesday

Today I was invited to lunch with Old Kemon and Maria. It was to be a welcome back occasion. Kemon and I sat at a table under the lemon tree while Old Maria busied herself in the tiny kitchen. The courtyard has room, apart from the lemon tree, for one or two tubs of geraniums and a small bed of rosemary and mint. A washing line stretches from the lemon tree to the far wall of the house, beneath which a glass-paned door leads into their bedroom. A little home dreamed about and longed for during thirty years in New York.

Kemon and I made polite conversation until Old Maria emerged with an oven dish of crusty brown potatoes and a leg of equally crusty browned lamb. We tucked in with a will (I had skipped most of my breakfast in readiness). Never have I tasted anything to compare with the old lady's cooking. I enquired the secret of the roast lamb. Kemon explained what had to be done. (The information as new, to him, perhaps, as it was to me.) First the meat was boiled for about an hour and only then was it put into the oven with plenty of oil, the potatoes absorbing the good flavour at the same time.

I staggered homewards with many *efkaristos* on my part and satisfied smiles from my hosts. Fortunately there had been no second course on offer.

Thursday

Unseasonable storms have hit the village.

'Did you hear they had an earthquake in Athens today?' Evagora called from her washing line. 'Number five on the scale and perhaps more to come.'

After the catastrophic earthquake in Turkey three weeks ago, these storms seem ominous. The village people have told us of the tremors they felt here some weeks before the quake hit Turkey, when we were still away. These tremors sent them scurrying outdoors with fright. The strong stone buildings shook like jellies but there appear to be no new cracks in the masonry, only old lesions from general wear and tear. They say in Paphos that a quake some years back caused loud roaring underground, like the sound of a train entering a tunnel! The water in a private swimming pool began rocking to and fro, from one end to the other as a preliminary to the quake itself, which damaged a few houses.

Friday

I attend church to celebrate the birthday of the Virgin Mary. The church is well filled, mostly by women. For the first time since we came here I get a Mona Lisa-like smile from the wife of the priest. Her feet are not troubling her so much today and she has forgone her carpet slippers. As I purchase my candle I am hoping that neither she nor the other servers will remove it before its time. On various occasions I have had to watch it being whisked away and thrown into the re-cycling box, a container of elaborate, gilded wrought ironwork. The box stands beside the cupboard where the bread knife etc. is stored. The re-cycling box, being stacked with half-used candles, bears testimony to the fact that few of us are getting our money's worth. When the service grows too long and tedious, the two or three servers, or sometimes a member of the congregation, can find diversion and a chance to stretch their legs, by leaving their seats to hurl out the candles, count the offertory (in full view of all of us) or do other useful jobs.

The large silver icon of the Virgin has been taken down from its prominent position on the iconostasis. The lace curtains that hide most of the Virgin's face throughout much of the year have been taken away. At a given moment we follow the icon outdoors and queue up, the men first, to bob beneath it. My back protests a little, there not being much headroom. Suddenly, a latecomer appears, a big man carrying his small son. The priest gestures severely. Hurry up! Father and child, the latter with egg on its bib, bob beneath the icon and then hurry home again to resume their interrupted breakfast.

Tuesday

This afternoon I went round to Old Crystalla with a bowl of jelly, but she was out. I found Old Demetri in his garden in conversation with a builder, who is restoring a neighbour's house. The builder obligingly translated for us and, feeling a bit foolish, I handed over the jelly. Demetri, slightly non-plussed, hurried indoors to put it in their tiny refrigerator, returning with a bowl of giant-sized figs. I accepted the figs graciously, conscious of the fact that Tim and I have already eaten half his crop, to say nothing of his sweet corn and his cucumbers.

Monday

Sitting this afternoon with Old Crystalla and daughter Maroulla under her grapevine, where a small restoring breeze blew, the women attempted to instruct me in another lesson in Greek. The old lady, her work-worn hands pressed to her knees with amusement, beamed through her thick glasses at my feeble efforts.

'*Ne. Ne. Cocoras! Cocoras!*'

As though they heard their names being called, the hens in the fowl yard next door set up a merry cackling. All three of us were so engrossed that we did not notice half a dozen people entering the garden. The party, draped with cameras, began moving about the courtyard. One of them produced a cine camera and, instructing the others to group themselves in front of the old well, began taking shots. They then broke away and wandered about, poking into this and that. The young man of the cine camera then strode to the grapevine under which we sat, and within a few feet of us began helping himself. He then offered grapes to a smartly turned out young woman, who appeared to be his wife. At no time did any of the party acknowledge our presence until, irritated by such rudeness, I asked them who they were. Old Crystalla and Maroulla were silent.

'*Ruske*,' they replied.

Immediately Maroulla was dispatched indoors to fetch figs and a giant bowl of grapes. All was enthusiasm and smiling cordiality. The figs disappeared. So did the grapes.

Rather primly I told the young man the Greek word for thank you is '*efkaristo*'.

'*Efkaristo! Efkaristo!*' More smiles all round.

'My mother is happy to see them,' Maroulla tells me when they have gone, but there is no reproach in her voice. Until the advent of her new Russian daughter-in-law, Evagora would have had a different reaction, methinks.

Tuesday

I called Thekla this morning. Help! The wc has blocked and disaster threatens.

Me: Shall I telephone the plumber? Ask Panyiotis?
Thekla: The plumber cannot come.
Me: Is he ill? (Familiar sinking of heart.)
Thekla: He is in the Army. Tassos is in the Army. *All* the men, they are in the Army.
Me: For how long?

They are there for three days. Well, that's better than one month, with the picking of the olives. She tells me that she will come herself. She does so and fixes the thing in a jiffy.

Friday

This evening, when I called to see Old Kemon and Maria, there was a stick propped against their gate discouraging entry. I decided to ignore it and went in. Both of them were in the front parlour, as usual, but surrounded by piles of fluffy cotton. There were bits of it stuck to trousers and black stockings, and for once Maria was so engrossed in her work she barely looked up. I joined in to help, plucking wads of the impacted cotton that had come from an old mattress, and then teasing it out.

'The rich people,' Kemon explained carefully as we worked, 'will send these things away to be done for them. But we are the poor people, so we do it ourselves!'

He mentioned places in town where you can take your old mattress, have its insides 'fluffed up' and returned to you in a matter of days, good as new.

'But this is good because we save money.'

Both old people beamed happily at the thought.

'We save ten pounds or maybe twelve!'

'Is it kapok?'

'This comes from the flower that grows. First the flower is nice and then it closes like this and it makes a nut like this.' He demonstrated with his hands to show the size of a walnut. 'Then when it gets dry inside it makes the cotton. This flower, it makes the flour for the bread.'

It was difficult to see quite how this works but Kemon, who likes to repeat himself, insists this flower also makes the flour for the bread. Be that as it may, we worked steadily on, Kemon getting a crick in his neck from the concentrated effort and a sore shoulder to boot. I began to sneeze.

210

'When I work I tell my wife she must pay me! Otherwise I go to the coffee shop!'

Heavy silence from Maria. 'This cotton,' he continued, 'is not so good as the wool. The wool, it is becoming from the hair of the sheep. In summer the people they cut the hair off here and here and here, all over the sheep. The wool, it makes a nice soft mattress which is warm in the winter. The cotton it is not so warm.'

On the spare bed in the parlour (the bed Kemon sat on when visitors came), our half-filled mattress lay ready to receive more of the reworked cotton. Underneath was a second mattress awaiting attention.

'How long has this taken you?'

'*Theftera, Triti, Tetarti, Pembti, Paraskevi.* Maybe we finish on *Savato,* Saturday!'

Both of them are so pleased with their efforts it is hard to tell what satisfies them more: the knowledge that several weeks' work will save them ten whole pounds, or maybe the possibility that newly stuffed mattresses might attract visits from their faraway daughters.

OCTOBER

Tuesday

I called on Harry today. Harry is harassed. He is restoring his father's house at Kato D—. Harry hails from New York. He left Cyprus for New York at the age of eighteen when it became apparent that his relatives were trying to marry him off. When his father told him he could have the family house in Kato D— if he agreed to marry Droulla, he told his father 'keep the house'. Now, some twenty years later, his father is dead, Droulla has long since given her heart elsewhere and Harry has the house.

Now in late October there are problems. Harry has been here all summer and the rains are coming but the roof has yet to be done.

'I'm listening ever day to the BBC forecasts. Oh my Gard. There are these storms coming to Cyprus from the west tomorrow. Do you know what this carpenter said to me yesterday? He said that the old flat village tiles I want are out of production and he can't get any more. He's got the *Portuguese* ones and the *Roman* ones, but not the flat *French* ones. Now, why didn't he tell me that months back? Why leave it till *now*? So I said to myself, wait a minute. A friend of mine owns the tile factory making these old tiles. I'll ring his daughter and find out. She tells me: Harry, it's true we have no tiles at the moment. I say, When will you have them? She says, Maybe in a couple of weeks. My Gard. I'm leaving in two weeks! I'll cancel my ticket and go later, in November. This other man, he quoted me five thousand pounds to do the roof and he tells me he does plastic guttering. I tell him I don't want anything plastic in my house, so he says I'll have to find the gutters myself. So I go up to Pano – to see this chap George I've known for thirty years. He makes all the gutters for the houses in Pano. Do you know what he quoted me? He wanted *thirty pounds* a metre for thirty metres of guttering! Now hold it, I told him. Are these gutters of yours made of *gold*, or something? You want thirty pounds a metre for pieces of gutter painted white and made of *tin*? So this other chap I found, he quotes me four thousand pounds for doing the roof, gutters included. *Not* plastic.'

'What state is your roof in at the moment, Harry?'

'The roof's off but they've put this plastic sheeting to stop the rain. Well, I just hope it does stop the rain. The locals are all pissed off at me as we all know they're praying for rain and there's me praying it won't. Last week I thought, I can't take any more of this stress, so when friends invited me over for corfee and it was a beautiful morning, I went. We're sitting there in Pano, having our corfee, and suddenly all these huge black clouds have come up! Oh my Gard. I said to my friends, This is no good, I can't relax. I'll have to go. So I drove down the mountain and peered at anywhere in the sky I could see *sun*. It seemed OK, so I headed towards Larnaca and lay on the beach. But I couldn't relax. So I called up my neighbour on my mobile. What's the weather doing up there, Crystalla? Is it raining? She tried to soothe me down. She knows me. Don't worry, Harry, she says. It's hardly raining at all. Well, only a bit! The road isn't even wet and the drains are empty. So I relaxed a bit. Then I got in the car and drove home and the roads started looking wet the higher I got, but not too bad. There was a message from a friend from Limassol on my answerphone: *Hi Harry. Sorry you were out when we dropped by. We got caught in a torrential storm up your way, so didn't wait.* I called this guy back and said, How bad was it? Don't worry, it didn't last more than about twenty minutes, he said. So I race upstairs to my bedroom and I turn on all the lights and get this torch and I'm peering at the ceiling looking for leaks.

'While the roof is down, I got this electrician over. I said to him, I want you to do the wiring *now* so that the cables will be hidden. No, no. He couldn't do it like that. It had to be done the old way, with all the wiring showing.

'Listen, I said. What is your name? Mr Andreas, he said. Mr

Andreas, I said, you don't know me, but what I have to tell you is that I must have everything purfect. Do you understand? So he came back yesterday all dressed up. In a suit! Can you grab that? His clothes were all *ironed*! I thought, Oh my Gard. Not one of *those*? Not the type who doesn't want to dirty his hands! Then I had a call and I went downstairs to answer the phone and I was only gone ten minutes and when I'd got back he'd done it! No problem. These people! I think I won't go back to New York; it's horrible in the winter. I haven't been on the beach here all summer! That really bugs me. I think I'll go to Sydney.'

'What about the floors. Are they OK now?'

'Don't tark to me! This chap – you know, the one who came over and said that they'd put the wrong stuff down between the tiles? They used plaster. It means when you wash them, damp works its way down. And then you've got the damp working its way up as well. So he said he'd sand them. Why did I let him do it? He turned up with this machine. I should have stopped him. The floors in the lobby and the sitting room are all shiny now. You know that nice *natural* look they had? Well, it's gorn! He's ruined them! And the dust! I had these two women in from the village and I had them cleaning up all day. The dust! It was about fifteen centimetres thick. Luckily I didn't let him go anywhere near the kitchen. And I was on my hands and knees for two days picking the plaster out between the tiles with a screwdriver. I said to this chap, I could have a more relaxing time doing a hard stint at the gym. My knees! He thought that kinda funny. Next time I'll have the whole lot up. Chuck 'em out. And find some more of the old ones. It'll cost me a packet.

'This roof man, the one who quoted me four thousand pounds, he's great. Really great. He had George come over. And George turns up, all downcast and sorry for himself. He has to work so hard. Why should he? You know the type. And this roof chap gives him the works. He was beginning to bother me, the way he went for George. Tarked to him as though he was a – a –'

'Peasant?'

214

'Yes, peasant. That's the word. So I got the chap on one side and I said, Should you be tarking to him quite like that, and he tells me it's the only way. And George, he's saying, Yes sir and no sir. Well, I've learnt a lesson *there*, that's for sure. I come back home to be *grounded*, Liz. I think I've been grounded enough for this year. I'm going!'

Friday

The moment of truth re our drains has arrived at last. There have been rumblings and grumblings for months and, as Thekla has shown no interest in spite of our pleas, Tim has done a certain amount of plunging with the plunger in the kitchen sink. However, he is not a plumber and strange smells have been wafting about for some time. I called up Kyriakos, the giant-sized fellow from the upper village (Cypriots, generally, are not tall). By some miracle he was able to turn up immediately this afternoon. He reported his findings: i.e., that a whole new drain extending across the courtyard is what is needed. We had reported this news to Thekla but got no positive response except 'You must do the work yourselves! You are living in the house,' etc. etc.

'I will tackle Thekla now,' said Tim, on his return this evening. He drove his Rover up the hill to The House of the Wind and was gone for at least two to three Keo beers' duration. However, the news was better. Thekla has relented and agreed to renew the main drain. This will mean disturbing yards of the concrete flooring in our courtyard and undoing all Tim's hard work with the paint brush.

Thursday

More days of smells have now gone by; nearly a week, in fact. No sign of Kyriakos. He can hardly be 'picking the olives' and if he is one of the island's fifty thousand 'hunters' (a misnomer, if ever there was one) this would only involve his absence on Wednesdays. It mystifies both Tim and me that these men can find anything to shoot. Wherever we go on the island, even through areas signposted somewhat euphemistically 'Nature Reserves', never a feather, let alone a bird attached to it, is to be seen. But come Sundays or Wednesdays throughout the winter, the braves are out on the hills. The small varieties of birds, including the migrating ones passing through, experience a much more cruel fate. They are caught on twigs that have been dipped in a treacle-like substance and die a slow and painful death, unless put out of their misery in time.

My letter to *The Cyprus Weekly* about this barbaric practice was never published. Politics? Would it have received attention if I had sent it to a Greek newspaper, written in that language? I doubt it.

Wednesday

My elder brother and his wife arrived last week en route for their home in New South Wales after a jaunt in Russia. The jaunt was a trip on the Trans-Siberian Railway. As they both have formidable intellectual interests that cover just about everything, I was feeling somewhat nervous about my rôle as tour guide. Instead of dealing with one Elephant's Child of I'satiable-curiosity, I would be coping with two.

The day arrived. Immediately upon alighting from the plane, my brother asked me what was the population of Cyprus – both Greek and Turkish – and what were the Greek and Turkish names for the island? I already felt too flustered to give reliable answers, and by the end of their short visit felt in some need of a stiff local brandy.

Needless to say, Kyriakos turned up the previous day and the courtyard was soon in a state of upheaval. We were all four of us

obliged to use the precipitous little staircase in the kitchen, 'hand made' by Tassos. The angle of the stairs is a shade less acute than that of a ladder. As the only entrance into the courtyard from the lane is through our front parlour, pipes, bags of cement, drilling equipment etc., were soon moving merrily about. All we needed was a good thunderstorm to add some mud to the chaos, but fortunately this held off.

The courtyard repairs drove us out of the house most days and our first visit was to Kourion, known to the Romans as Curium. These ruins stretch for acres over a massive rock face two hundred and thirty feet above the sea. They date from Hellenistic, Roman and Early Christian times, and there is much more of the Early Kingdom still underground. By the end of our inspections even my relatives began to look as though they would be happy to leave the latter where it is. Twisting our necks to read the Latin inscriptions on some wonderfully preserved mosaic floors gave all three of us headaches in the end. We sank down on the stone seating in the amphitheatre (relatively small by Roman standards), perched as it is on the cliffs with a vast backdrop of shoreline and sea. Here Tim and I had watched a local production of *As You Like It* one summer evening recently. The acoustics are superb. Now, in late October, great cloudscapes of battleship greys, slashed by sudden shafts of sunlight, lit up Kourion's honey-coloured stonework of broken columns, crumbling walls and pediments. An exquisitely carved shell, part of a drinking fountain, lay by itself near a path. Here I was able to explain to my visitors the difference between these Greek and Roman columns, to wit, that while the former have shafts that are grooved vertically, the latter are fluted with winding threads. This piece of information was accepted without question and we pressed on.

There were fine mosaics of fighting gladiators, and in a Roman villa more mosaics, depicting the legend of Achilles, whose mother had tried to prevent him going to the Trojan War by dressing him in women's clothes. (Presumably, at this stage, Achilles was below the age of consent.) Dipping in and out amongst the

218

centuries we identified the remains of a huge Christian basilica with 'deacon's rooms' and private rooms for the bishop nearby. At another private house (fifth century BC) the builder, whose name was Eustolios, was privileged enough to have had Apollo as his patron. This was where it all began to get muddling, where we started to get our headaches. Eustolios was clearly a BC Greek, but when the Romans took over they turned his house into public baths. Then Christian influences began to creep in, the mosaic floors now depicting floral and geometric designs with birds, animals and fish instead of portraits of people. What happened to the baths?

At this point we decided to stretch our necks and went to find the Sanctuary of Apollo Hylates. Two tall columns, with a pediment above, gave us the chance to look skywards. Apollo Hylates was a 'Greek import' and was worshipped only in Cyprus. A passage led from the Sanctuary to the Temple of Apollo himself (approximately seventh century BC).

An aquaduct brought water from the mountains for the Romans. The Greeks seemed to have got by with a massive cistern – or did they? Our guide book did not make this clear. At any rate, we returned home after a good day out but aware that, in spite of early earthquakes and the passage of time, there was a great deal of Kourion left to see – both overground and one day, perhaps underground.

The next visit was inland and northwards to Kykko monastery, where the erstwhile Makarios III had once been a twelve-year-old novice and later its abbot. This, fortunately, is not the sole reason for its fame, which is spread throughout the whole Orthodox world. Here there is a celebrated icon of the Madonna, said to have been painted by St Luke himself! The monastery buildings are relatively new, fires having destroyed it on several occasions, and it is altogether a place that breathes wealth rather than sanctity. A good deal of this wealth came from unfortunate farmers who bequeathed their land to the Church in order to relieve themselves of the heavy taxes the Church imposed on them. Kykko was thus able to invest in land not only in Cyprus but in Asia Minor and even Russia. It also owns valuable building land in Nicosia.

Coming home, we passed through the beautiful Cedar Valley, the trees being unique to Cyprus and larger than the Cedars of Lebanon. This valley is the last habitat of this marvellous tree and lies at the foot of Mount Trpylos. While tourism is quietly (and unquietly) wrecking much of the island's coastline, one can only hope that the Troodos will save itself. Certainly one or two very unhelpful roads that wind upwards from the coast can lead the visitor on a merry dance. Yesterday I took my relatives on a road that led innocently northwards from near Paphos. We drove on. The road narrowed and the bends got bendier. The views were spectacular, so much so that we barely noticed that at length our journey was ending in someone's back yard. In fact, it was a pleasure to find something so truly rustic, so hidden away and lost among its surroundings. The owner of the yard came out to greet us and did his best to re-direct us homewards, our map bearing little relationship to fact.

Friday

We waved my brother and sister in law off yesterday, one of them clutching a booklet entitled *Greek in Easy Stages*, and the other *A History of the Crusades* in paperback – three volumes.

NOVEMBER

Monday

Today there was a call from the artistic director's wife in Nicosia. The wardrobe mistress, who is coming from England especially to help our production, wishes to have my vital statistics. Me, a mere member of the chorus! Not in my whole life has a wardrobe mistress asked for my vital statistics or have I had a message from the wife of an artistic director. My bosom swelled with such pride I am in danger of giving her false information.

Our production of *Dick Whittington* will run for two weeks in early December. Rehearsals have already started. Taking pity on my misguided enthusiasm, the director, Jim, has put me in the chorus, although I tell him that I cannot sing for nuts. There is to be a harem scene, among others, in which I hope to be heavily veiled. Quite why we are singing 'What Shall We Do with the Drunken Sailor' is not yet clear. I feel somewhat like the Mother Superior in *The Sound of Music*. The other members of the chorus all look horribly young and fresh-faced and treat me with a depressing deference.

Wednesday

Tim and I have decided to spend Christmas in Egypt. Two days in Cairo, a week on the Nile and a quick overland jaunt to the Red Sea! Having had, all my life, a passionate interest in ancient Egypt, I enrolled some years ago in an adult education class in Egyptology. This, although much looked forward to, proved a disappointment. The pharaohs were all so muddling, except, of course, the flamboyant ones. I should have done the course years and years ago when the brain was young and fertile. My passion for Egyptian history has not waned, however, and next

Christmas will be a new start. Ah, Ozymandias, here we come.

Thursday

The weather is more unsettled now, with winter around the corner. Rainy days, though welcome, do not suit the aesthetics of our village and its surroundings. The warm, creamy stonework of the houses that sparkles in sunlight turns a dull pale umber, as does the pretty stonework along the lanes. So does the landscape. The leaves on our grapevine are browning and falling rapidly and must be swept off the roof terrace before they block the gutters and clutter the lane. I am thankful for our twice-weekly pantomime rehearsals which have started in Nicosia.

Monday

The wardrobe mistress tells us that there are to be three costume changes, the most exotic, for those of us in the chorus, being for the harem scenes. She has enveloped me in floating layers of tulle, up to the neck and down to ankles and wrists. The young things, mostly Cypriots, who make up the rest of the chorus have a good deal more bare flesh on show, mostly around the midriff. My veil is a godsend.

The setting for our *Dick Whittington* story was Famagusta until someone suggested that, as Greek sensibilities must be taken into account, the location should be changed. It was. At our rehearsal some weeks ago, the cast found themselves transported with great suddenness to Morocco. Why Morocco, none of us quite knew. In scene two, however, now dressed as a cockney flower seller in mob cap and skirts, I found myself doing the Lambeth Walk with the best of them. Those of us who had missed one of the rehearsals had not been given the new song sheets, and an Australian businessman (a fine baritone) led off with 'Yes We Have No Bananas' at a tender moment when the Sultan was about to greet his Sultaness (a dark-eyed local beauty), or was she his number one odalisque? Our director, an Englishman, seems immune to unhelpful suggestions coming from the cast. He sits in the front row. Perhaps it is as well, on occasion, that from the back of the stalls the words are fairly inaudible anyway. Last night we had a near miss when one of the Sultan's bodyguards all but decapitated one of the harem in an exuberant display of swordsmanship. She, a pretty little thing in her teens, was led off weeping quietly into her veil. However, she cheered up when the director suggested we switched to the final part of scene two, when, still in our veils, we rehearsed our favourite exit singing 'Wish Me Luck as You Wave Me Goodbye'. This requires us to file off stage with Fred Astaire-like hand waves and is rendered with great gusto by one and all. Most of the chorus are far too young to appreciate the pathos of the song and its meaning. This is left to the one and only grandparent on stage.

Wednesday

Our production is to be held next weekend at the Russian Cultural Centre in Nicosia, which does not supply us with any heating. As winter has set in, we are forced to do costume changes in arctic conditions. Whipping in and out of our outfits in record time, we struggle with yashmaks that need pinning, floating pieces of chiffon that refuse to stay tucked and flower sellers' skirts and bodices that refuse to zip up. The Good Fairy, who has trouble with her wings, wand and blonde wig, gets in everyone's way in our cramped quarters. There is a certain amount of suppressed resentment that the said Fairy (a buxom lady) is allowed far more than her fair share of time in the make-up room. Some of the less charitable among us can see why. There are many and varied faces to be either improved or transformed and time is of the essence. The first night is next Friday and things are reaching fever pitch. Dick Whittington himself has thrown one or two tantrums. A tall, strikingly good-looking young woman with a superb figure, she has been found, on occasion, slumped in the wings, missing her cue. Only a good deal of flattery coming from the Sultan and his bodyguards and some cajoling by her mother have persuaded her to continue. We all have to admit that in her long boots, tight breeches and cocked hat she cuts a handsome dash. Her cat, a slightly built girl, is far easier to deal with and a most effective dancer. But she has no pretensions to stardom, unlike her master.

Tim has come to one or two rehearsals, puffing on his new find of pencil-slim cigars. His doctor has recommended them as less harmful than cigarettes! An obliging taverna down the valley orders them in for him. As they are more expensive than cigarettes, he imagines that he is economizing by cutting them in half.

DECEMBER

Wednesday

Dick Whittington was a sell-out on our four nightly shows and two matinées. Profits will go to a school for disadvantaged children.

As members of the cast began going down with a severe strain of flu halfway through the performances, the process hurried on by our chilly costume changes, it soon became a matter of all hands on deck. I myself missed the last performance. Our wardrobe mistress found herself in the chorus and one of the scene shifters ended up as a member of the Sultan's bodyguard. The Sultan himself stayed the course, using Tim's Egyptian fly whisk to great effect.

The Australian High Commissioner, a jolly bachelor, graciously allowed me to stay at the Commission residence over the weekend, to save me having to drive home between shows. He was prepared to risk the dangers to which he might have put his reputation had a lady from the harem been spotted entering his premises at dead of night.

Saturday

Evagora has been instructed about care of the lovebirds. I think she regards our concern for them as somewhat eccentric, but she is a good-hearted soul. I had thought of asking Androulla if she would cope (she does not have four strapping sons to feed), but the sheer business of explaining birds, dustbins, front door key etc., in Greek, seemed hardly worth the effort.

JANUARY 2000

Monday

Back home again. Our Egyptian venture lived up to all expectations, apart from a certain pharaoh-fatigue setting in. This happened somewhere between the Temple of Horus at Edfu and those at Abu Simbel. Our excellent guide, Khaled, in spite of his own personal ordeal with shuffling his tourists about during Ramadan, did his best to enlighten us about all things pharaoh. As we tottered about Queen Hatshepsut's Temple and then on to those at Karnak, (having done the pyramids pretty thoroughly beforehand), we longed to hear something of the lives of the ordinary, humdrum, everyday Egyptian. Eventually, we discovered a passenger on the sun deck of our boat where a pleasant hour or two passed in her company. She was a mild-mannered young woman who, it transpired, had hired a horse at one point of our voyage and galloped off into the desert. While the rest of our party had trekked off after Khaled to study the art of papyrus making, she had visited villages and hobnobbed with the locals.

Yes, the women of ancient Egypt were on an equal footing with the men, she told us and as she turned out to be a student of archaeology, we saw no reason to disbelieve her. Women had the same legal as well as social rights, the same salaries and wages. Both sexes wore make-up, the black eyeliner producing an anti-glare effect as do our modern sunglasses. Make-up was considered so important that there is a recorded incident where workers went on strike for it as well as for moisturizing oils. Hair was cropped against lice and the rich wore wigs as well as perfuming their hair, which was dyed with henna. The workers enjoyed a nourishing diet of dried fish, salads, barley bread and barley beer. The rich ate duck cooked in honey and drank wine.

Various wise pieces of advice appear among the ancient writings: 'Let your eye observe in silence and you will see your wife's skill'

226

227

or 'do not boss her'. 'Be merry. Toil no more than is required,' advises one sage. To the ancient Egyptians heaven was Egypt. Small wonder then, that those who could afford it wished to take as much as they could with them into the next world. For the impoverished rural Egyptian little has changed over the centuries which, for the visitor, gives a magical timelessness to a slow journey down the Nile.

Back in Cairo, we were able to explore the Museum. Here, days, even weeks, could be spent with much profit although the place needs a thorough dusting. For a few extra pounds we were able to inspect some of the royal mummies where our friend, Rameses II, moulders beside one of his (Nubian) wives. His aquiline features and delicate hands bear little resemblance to his general demeanour at Abu Simbel where an exaggerated account of his victories in Syria against the Hittites is depicted on the vast temple walls (1270 BC) Rameses had the prudence to marry a Hittite princess, taking ancient Palestine for himself while the Hittites took Syria. In the Cairo Museum nothing remains of any 'sneer of cold command'.

We saw in the New Millennium in Cairo. On the streets that night, the milling throngs reduced our progress to a shuffle. Along the bridges young men perched on the balustrades like swallows, shoulder to shoulder, greeting all who passed with cheerful cries. 'Happy Christmas, Mrs Clinton' one of them shouted. We responded. No sign was there of the women, except a few tucked away in passing cars. The night was balmy. The sky glowed with crystal stars. The old river flowed silently onwards, carrying away another less than glorious century into the bosom of the Mediterranean.

Wednesday

Old Demetri next door has lost his plough. On my visits down the hill to visit Madonna I passed that plough, lying against his orchard fence as it has done for decades, its simple wooden design belying the strenuous toil that man and beast endured. Now, someone has perhaps seen its potential as an 'arty' object for display in some trendy taverna down on the coast.

'Yes, that's how they used to plough in the old days. By hand and donkey (laughter). But we've moved on here in Cyprus, you know, like everywhere else.'

There are so few burglaries in our village. A friend here recently left her front door open by mistake. On her return a week later everything was as before. But Old Demetri is in shock and sorrow.

Sunday

A knock on our door this morning and there is Eleonora hotfoot from church and bearing yet another home-made cake (very rich-looking and fruity). My heart sinks. She is inside the parlour before I can gather my wits about me. She wishes to speak to both of us on a matter of some urgency and the fruit cake is her way of clinching the matter. I call to Tim, who is upstairs. He appears and we progress to the sitting room, where Eleonora settles herself in the best chair, the only armchair, and we take our places on the hard orange ones. The fruit cake is already in the kitchen, non-returnable. She is adamant that we make up our minds about her father-in-law's house down the lane in which, some six months ago, we had expressed an interest. She must have our answer *now*, today. The fact that, in a very rash moment, we had paid her (and her husband, cousins and aunts) a goodly deposit on the house but had since had second thoughts about its purchase did not mollify her one jot. What is more, she knows that we know no other offers for the house have been made. She knows and we know that the cost of restoring the crumbling old pile will be exorbitant, which was the reason why, in saner moments, we had backed off the idea, at some considerable loss to ourselves. The deposit is non-refundable. If anyone should be put out it is Tim and me, but we know we were foolish, she knows we were foolish and we all know that the house is a white elephant of gigantic proportions. However, Eleonora is a business woman and it isn't for nothing that she owns several apartment blocks down on the coast where her rents are eyebrow-raising.

Ah, but the white elephant has magnificent views! This was our undoing. Magnificent views and a giant-sized lemon tree that shades most of its courtyard. It also has a fig. After paying our deposit so rashly, we would hurry over every day or two to water that fig and a few struggling vines. This all had to be done with buckets carried from a tap outside the kitchen. The father-in-law had lived, as so many elderly Cypriots do, in great hardship with no modern conveniences of any kind, save for a decrepit wc on the opposite side of the courtyard to his bedroom. An old iron bedstead of great antiquity, a Van Gogh rush chair, a few mouldering books and an icon or two on the walls were his only furnishings here. The kitchen is equally basic, with one cold water tap and a cooking stove of 1920s vintage. Up the courtyard steps we trod that first day and greeted the view, or rather the view greeted us. Ayios Maria stands a short distance ahead and beyond is the panorama we have grown to love in its familiarity and beauty. There is one very large room on this top floor and potential for the building of extra rooms. It was all very expensively tempting...

We are eating the fruit cake but Eleonora is not pleased.

FEBRUARY

Monday

Chrisso, the wife of our mukhtar, broke her leg last month. The village support group went into action immediately. While Chrisso lies on a day bed in her front parlour, Koulla, Evagora and others bustle about with her chores. No danger here that the mukhtar will have to soil his hands with the washing up, cooking, sweeping etc. His life goes on without a ripple. Meanwhile Chrisso, whose front doors are made of glass, can keep in touch with the world passing by outside.

Tuesday

Our High Commissioner friend tells me that my Christmas card design of angels flying over the Sydney Opera House, which he dispatched at Christmas as his official greeting card, has gone down well. Five rather plump angels rise upwards from Lavender Bay on the harbour's north shore, their wings shaped like the sails of the Opera House.

I am finishing an oil painting of the view from our church of Ayios Maria. The scene is sunrise, which has meant some early starts for me, not so easy at this time of year. I can balance my canvas on the stone wall that skirts the church, thus deleting the need for my easel. What colours go into that sky? Lemon and cadmium yellow, a touch of cadmium red, merging into soft Prussian blues. Very difficult. The foreground drops away sharply into valleys and plateaus of raw sienna dotted with the blue-green of olive, the dark green of carob and the paler almond trees. The hills fold backwards into distances of smudgy Prussian blues. All too soon the sun has popped up, the sky becomes brighter, the landscape sharper...

231

Wednesday

Madonna has joined me in being in bad odour again with Father S. It is comforting to have an accomplice in guilt.

She escaped from her yard today and was found wandering happily up the lane by the olive press. I took her by the halter and led her homewards, our route, to avoid circumnavigating the whole village, taking us past the church. Halfway across its precincts, we were both of us startled by an angry bellow. It came from the doorway in the tower, where our priest, somewhat surprisingly, appeared to be waving a broom. Leaning on this, he gave another shout, louder and angrier than the first, and followed this up with vigorous gesticulations, which obliged him to let go of the broom. It fell with a clatter.

Madonna, unable to retaliate, remained mute. I tried a few helpless shrugs and what I hoped looked like an apology, while only able to guess at the tribulations being wished upon our heads. I pointed an accusing finger at Madonna. Father S pointed an accusing finger back. At last donkey and I decided the whole business was getting us nowhere, so we hurried homewards. By the gate into her yard, I lifted the tarpaulin from the stack of parsley hay and removed an armful of it in a gesture of camaraderie. Guilt did not dampen her appetite and she set to with a will.

Thursday

The 'unholy row' between the Bishop of Limassol and the Bishop of Paphos continues. The latter has accused the former of undesirable sexual practices, and an investigation into these allegations will shortly decide whether or not there is any substance to them. One of the accusers is a hairdresser. If so, the popular Bishop of Limassol will be defrocked. He is credited with reviving flagging church attendances and is very much a man of the people.

Meantime the Bishop of Paphos is a more worldly character

with keen business acumen. Rumour has it that the luxury hotel built in one of the island's few remaining nature reserves in the Akamas has a strong flavour of Bishop in the pie.

The popular Bishop of Limassol sees these accusations as a plot to spoil his chances in the Byzantine struggle for a successor to the ailing Archbishop of Limassol. He has called on his flock to 'stay calm, forgive the misguided and pray for the storm to pass. This is a tragedy and a shame'. He says, 'While our political leaders are struggling in New York to counter Turkish demands, the Church is preoccupied with these petty matters.'

Monday

Diana and Ralph have returned. We tried to explain that Cyprus in February is cold but Diana replied firmly, 'Not as cold as England.' She has taken an apartment down on the coast where, admittedly, the temperatures are higher and the sunshine more reliable. We wished she had asked for our assistance in this as she and Ralph are paying an extortionate rent for what they are getting. The apartment is minky (a favourite word of my mother's) and worse still, the building is situated in a sea of builder's rubble. This is not good for either of them, Diana with her bad hip and Ralph with his poor eyesight.

The morning after their arrival Ralph was sent off at nine o'clock with a shopping list for Woolworths, while Diana sorted out the apartment and the unpacking. Lunchtime came and as there was no sign of Ralph, Diana had hers. After lunch she had her siesta and then made a cup of tea. At four o'clock she rang us.

'I've lost Pa,' she said.

'What do you mean *lost*?'

'Well, he's not here. He hasn't come back.'

Tim took off for the coast forthwith. Fortunately it was a Saturday. The story unfolded thus:

Ralph had found Woolworths – it was not far from the apartment – and had also found the bits and pieces of provender that Diana had written on her shopping list. However, once out of doors again, he became disorientated. He is now in his eighty-fifth year and besides, he had a spot of jet lag. On top of these difficulties, he had forgotten their address. Consequently he wandered about with his shopping bags while the morning drifted by and lunchtime came. At this point he felt tired and sat on the esplanade, looking at the sea. Finally, he hailed a taxi.

'Where do you want to go?' asked the driver.

'I don't know,' replied Ralph.

The taxi driver took his passenger to the police station, whence Tim eventually collected him.

Diana produced shepherd's pie for dinner that evening, as a celebration of Ralph's safe return. The apartment kitchen equipment does not run to a potato masher but she managed the job with a fork. It was a pity, though, that Ralph had bought a tin of tuna chunks in brine when she was sure she had written *tuna in oil* on her list.

235

MARCH

Monday

The 6th March, the first day of the Lenten fast. Chrisso invited me into her kitchen for coffee. Her leg is now out of plaster. She showed me what will be her daily fare for the next five weeks — vegetables, fruit and salads. Then, with a shy laugh, she opened the fridge door. An appetizing leg of lamb lay within. The mukhtar needs strengthening at all seasons. That is understood.

Monday

I am behind with the diary. Tim has broken his arm from a fall on the courtyard steps. After rain, the steps become extra slippery. Nicos took us to the Larnaca hospital yesterday, where Tim was handed over to a surly foreign doctor in Outpatients. The whole business took hours and the off-hand rudeness of the doctor filled me with a misgiving which was reinforced when Tim appeared with his forearm encased in a heavy and very cumbersome plaster. Nicos kindly drove us home again.

Friday

Tim's arm is giving him a lot of pain. His thumb and fingers are swollen and blue and the plaster is very uncomfortable. Nothing will persuade him to return to the hospital, however, in case he meets the same doctor. He agreed to be taken to the cottage hospital in the upper village today, where the situation was said to be satisfactory. We are not so sure.

Saturday

It is said that three thousand people have been invited to the wedding of Androulla and Ileas' son. They are near neighbours of ours, Androulla having been so helpful with the gas cylinder episode in our early days here.

At four o'clock this afternoon there was a stir outside in the lane and I spotted Old Crystalla and her daughter Maroulla distributing small cakes and glasses of cordial to anyone who was interested. The bridegroom was being shaved and got ready by his best man. This is the custom.

After some forty minutes or so the music of violins brings us all scurrying outdoors again. The musicians lead the small procession through the village, the bridegroom immaculate in dark blue suit and hair, Beatles-style, reaching to his collar. The best man behind him has hair halfway down his back. Last come six little bridesmaids in fluffy pink dresses, their hair swept up into tight little chignons and set off with the traditional coronets of waxed orange blossom. We flatten ourselves against the walls to allow the procession to pass. It is all very solemn. We sit in Crystalla's garden until it is time to get ourselves ready too. Old Demetri announces that he would like to go to the wedding. After some discussion Maroulla tells her father that he will have to stay behind. Old Crystalla's heart is not good, in spite of her operation. Demetri acquiesces good-naturedly.

The church service is in the upper village. The village is a good deal larger than ours yet the magnificence of its church surprises the newcomer. Twelve giant crystal and gold chandeliers cast a soft glow over the congregation and over the bridal couple as they enter, hand in hand. During the ceremony, which lasts over an hour, the young couple stand like statues while small children dart about, pushchairs rock the babies and the congregation chatters. The officiating priest, a good deal shorter than the bride and groom, has difficulty in getting the double crowns in place. The bride, taller than the groom, bends forward to help the

237

proceedings but too late to prevent her elegant chignon from being all but dislodged as the old priest, almost on tiptoe now, squashes the crown on to her head. He holds it there for several moments. Both crowns are joined by a white ribbon in symbolic bond. This part of the ceremony now over, the young couple process three times around a table in the central aisle on which the bride's and bridegroom's mothers have placed offerings of little cakes. This is a signal for the congregation to disperse. Some of us line up to present the young couple with our monetary offerings, discreetly placed inside envelopes.

The last wedding breakfast we attended being too much of a bunfight for our liking, we decide to forgo this one and wend our way homewards. Tim is not in the mood, anyway. Suddenly a voice from a passing car bellows, 'Aren't you two coming to the feast?' It is Nicos.

'No. We've got another engagement,' we fib.

'Shame. I was going to keep seats for you at our table! I don't hold with all that religious stuff in the church. You must be crazy. The feast is the best part.'

Back home, I remember Old Demetri. I send him off to the feast and sit with Crystalla. Tim has gone to rest his arm.

Saturday

To distract Tim from his painful arm, we decided today to make a second attempt to visit the monastery of Ayios Minas. It is, in fact, a convent, founded in the fifteenth century. Some years back we were halted in our tracks by a sign on the main gateway forbidding entry to all females wearing trousers and all males who were not. As I was in trousers and Tim was in shorts, we had turned away. Had we known it, the nuns provide sarongs for the unsuitably clothed. These hang on a rail outside the little shop by the inner gates. Today I wore a skirt and Tim his yellow trousers, Tim reckoning that the nuns might appreciate a spot of colour.

238

The road as you approach the monastery winds through a little valley of unexpected greenness, soothing to the eyeballs on this white and rocky island. A sign here announces that the area is a game reserve, but not so much as a rabbit or pheasant did we spot amongst the willows, poplars and lush eucalyptus. The fifty thousand huntsmen have done a thorough job, but whatever wildlife that is left will now have a respite until October.

The monastery's caretaker, a solitary male, occupies a tiny cottage outside the gates. His name is George and he has followed his daughter from England. George is a widower and his only daughter a nun here.

The wondrous hush that one grows to expect in these places filters through the cloistered garden, where the scent of jasmine haunts the senses. Trailing geraniums and petunias sprout from giant wine and olive jars. Trays of herbs lie drying in the sun.

George showed us into the ancient chapel and then sent us upstairs through more cloisters where we found the elderly nun who paints the icons. George was right: she had finished her candle making and, it now being three o'clock, she was seated at her easel, executing delicate strokes with a fine brush and a deft hand. As she worked she talked, her apple red cheeks glowing as much from health as from the heaviness of her vestments. Her little pots of powdered colours were arranged before her, the egg yolk added to the tempera to bind the paint. All the colours, she explained, come from the good earth of this island, ground fine and pure. At the moment she is working on a large icon of the Virgin and Child, the Byzantine influence reflected in the expressionless features of the subjects and the stiff and formal treatment of the drapery.

Downstairs in the little shop we bought a small triptych, hand painted, of St George and his inevitable dragon, the Virgin and Child and an unknown Saint with quite a pleasant expression. We bought also a pot of the convent's famous home-produced honey.

Tuesday

It looks as if Father S has forgiven me. Today as his utility truck passed my Mazda in the lane, he going uphill, I going down, I was rewarded with a cheerful '*kalimera*' and a smile that sliced in half his massive beard.

Thursday

I am having some physiotherapy myself. Empathy for Tim's painful arm has triggered my painful back! I drove to Nicosia to the Hilton Hotel, where Natasha, pummelling and massaging me today, pieced together the story of her life since she left Russia some six years ago. Now, the love story part of it is over and she must fly to Algeria soon to get a divorce.

She was living in Paris, when she met and fell in love with an Algerian student. They married, but when she became pregnant the high costs of giving birth in a French hospital became a problem for them. Natasha's sister-in-law, a doctor, suggested that they come to Algeria for the birth. She could advise and help them. This they did. However, Natasha was unprepared for the anti-Western sentiment that greeted her. Leaving her hotel one day, the young Russian was shouted at and kicked in the stomach by Algerian police. On hearing that her husband had married a foreigner, they then confiscated his passport. Natasha miscarried a four-month-old child and was forced to leave the country alone. She convalesced in Austria before finding her way to Cyprus and a job. Now she works as a masseuse at one of Nicosia's leading hotels. Her savings go towards supporting two nephews at university in Nicosia and eleven relatives in Russia. One of them, her sister, she is bringing to Cyprus for a holiday. Meanwhile, a young Cypriot wants to marry her.

'But I love Ali,' Natasha confesses as she slaps more oil onto her palms. 'How shall I decide?'

'Perhaps when you return to Algeria you will know for certain, about your Cypriot, I mean. Is it safe for you to go back?'

'I go for a divorce, yes. I cannot stay in Algeria. Ali, he must stay. They have taken his passport.'

The inevitability of it all bears down on us as Natasha moves across to put on a Tchaikovsky symphony on her cassette player. We listen to it in silence.

Friday

Thekla's son Chris and his wife, plus the new baby, are emigrating to England. They will join a relative who runs a fish and chip shop in Birmingham. Thekla is desolate at the forthcoming loss. The baby lies in its cot in a corner of the restaurant kitchen, a cot vacated by Thekla Junior not so long ago. Her grandmother divides her attention between baby and multitudinous culinary duties. Over a cup of strong Cyprus coffee Thekla tells me of her sorrow. I commiserate as best I can. Being a mother can be hard but being a grandmother even harder! At least Stella and her family are not leaving, I remind her. Her husband Andreas, a refugee from Northern Cyprus, has tried other parts of the world and announces firmly that this is the best place for rearing children. He found Australia altogether too large. Families were split. His wife agrees. Hard work seven days a week, Stella in her lace shop, Andreas holding down two jobs and the restaurant work on top of that, has earned them a fine house throbbing with modern conveniences and brand new furniture. Stella, as she drives her children to the village school in her shiny Vitari, does not need to reflect on her mother's childhood. Then there was foot slogging to school up hot and dusty roads, three times a day, there and back. And after school, the compulsory lace-making for the daughters before they were allowed out to play. One doubts whether Stella's daughter, Thekla Junior, will knuckle down to lace-making like her forebears.

241

APRIL

Saturday

Tim has gone to England! The situation with his arm having got worse, rather than better, we decided he must get a second opinion and quickly. There was barely time for him to say goodbye. The village people were surprised and sad. They have grown fond of their Timotheos and will miss the sight and sound of his Rover grinding up the mountain, the flags of Cyprus and Britain mounted on the front mudguards. Life will not be quite the same without the sight of their lanky friend striding through the lanes in his canary-yellow trousers and brown fedora, the latter worn in most weathers. If not the fedora, then the fake panama, but always the hat. Evagora came hurrying in with a gift of her home-made yoghurt.

'You'll sleep well back in England,' she joked. 'No more guns going off and barking dogs.'

'Perhaps the silence will keep me awake.'

On the way down the mountain we met Nicos. 'Jesus Christ, Tim! You're not going to a British hospital, are you? That National Health Service over there will be the death of you! You need your head read, my boy! Terrible stories they tell me about it. There was this chap got food poisoning and was dead in a week. Only went in there for an ingrown toenail, poor chap.'

'Sorry, Nicos. We've got to get to the airport.'

'I'll look after Liz. Don't worry about her.'

'Thanks!' Tim yelled back. 'I'll appreciate that.'

Monday

The International Law Conference for the Year 2000 opened in Nicosia today but Tim, the brains behind it, is missing!

Tuesday

I attended the Law Conference today. Tim had 'chosen' Cyprus for its geographical position at the confluence of three continents, Europe, Africa and the Middle East stretching into Asia. Feeling a little like a fish out of water but nevertheless keen to represent Tim and report back, I listened to one of the keynote addresses. The speaker reiterated to the five hundred or so delegates present that those from countries that practised the Common Law (such as Britain, the United States and the British Commonwealth) should here gain a better understanding and appreciation of the world's different legal systems. (The 'Balkan Corridor', being recently freed from the Eastern Bloc, was one. At this point my mind wandered a bit, to Roz and her hefty Balkan Bar admirer, Zorba the Greek etc.) The legal delegates present are of course sharp enough to appreciate the advantages of being here, of the opportunities offered to meet with their counterparts from competing legal systems.

Among subjects to be covered at the five-day conference are Environmental Law, International Trade, Ethics and Human Rights, Maritime Shipping, European Union.

I drove home feeling sad that Tim was missing it all but hoping that the notes I had scribbled in longhand might cheer him on his long sessions at the Rehabilitation Clinic.

Wednesday

Tim rang to say that he is fortunate to be able to attend the above-mentioned clinic, for it is close by his parents' home and is the only one in the country run by the National Health Service. Diana is boosting his morale with her 'diplomatic' recipes from countries far and wide, while he and Ralph are enjoying their sundowners together. (Perhaps this should be altered to raindowners?)

Tim's prognosis is difficult at this stage. He is having daily

243

physiotherapy, there being very little movement in his right thumb and forefinger. Fortunately the fracture is not on his good arm. In addition to his broken arm, the doctors have discovered some chipping of the bone in his shoulder.

Thursday

Anna has a new cook at her hotel – a Russian. Not only is she an excellent cook but a masseuse as well. On her afternoons off I have enjoyed a wonderful hour of her expertise as, doused with fragrant oils, I let myself luxuriate beneath Nina's healing hands. Are all Russians called Nina? What has happened to her namesake? Is she out of gaol by now and has she had her teeth out? Nina, the cook, is a large warm-hearted soul who wears her heart on her sleeve. As a spy, she would never pass the first post. Her only son, her pride and joy, has just arrived here from Moldova for two weeks' holiday. The young man is jobless and Nina, a divorcee, has come to Cyprus to earn the bread and butter. I drove them to the coast today for a swim. Nina's joy was touching. After my swim, I sat on the cliff top in Costas' garden and watched the pair of them sporting in the water for hour after hour, unable to get enough of it. The sun beat down without mercy but they had the sea and I had the gentle coastal breeze that springs up in the afternoons as regularly as clockwork.

On the way home we stopped at the small dress shop at the foot of our mountain. Its repertoire is decidedly limited but we found a suitable pair of jeans for Ivan and one or two shirts. Nina made several attempts to accommodate her generous frame into some shiny nylon blouses more suitable to night-clubbing than anything else. I have decided to take her to Larnaca for a shopping spree at the next opportunity.

Saturday

I woke today to a glorious spring morning, the lovebirds having woken me extra early with their chirpings. These dawn choruses have irritated one or two English guests who, used to rising at a later hour, have not always realized the benefit of greeting the dawn with cups of tea on the roof terrace. Today was sad in spite of birds and sunshine. Tim has gone and his canary yellow trousers hang in Thekla's mother's wardrobe and his plastic panama hat hangs on his peg by the front door. The fedora, of course, went to England. His fractured arm has brought some sobering thoughts to mind for both of us. Tim could be attending treatment for months, according to the specialists, and his shoulder might need an operation once the other remedial work is done.

Monday

The realization that we must leave the island has hit me badly. Somehow, against all reasoning, I had hoped for a stay of execution, so to speak. The place, warts and all, has grown on me. I realize, however, that it is not Tim's cup of perfect tea, his need to have his finger at all times on the pulse of world affairs being paramount. However, he has taken to the village and its people and they to him.

Thekla will have to be told about our departure, but her house is not hers any longer. It is ours. The rooms are full of us, of our ideas. The ferns by the aviary nearly reach the boughs of the loquat tree now. The blue plumbago vies for attention among both bougainvillaeas. Pots stand about on the roof terrace, softening its ugly corners. I am beginning to feel like Kipling's Roman Centurion: 'I have none other home than this, nor any life at all!' He, of course, was leaving Britain after a forty-year stint, not returning to it after only three.

I sat this evening on the roof terrace. I will still be here for

245

Easter, and this is a comfort. In fact, it will take a goodish time to leave. So much packing. So much organizing.

Sunday

I must decide about the fate of our lovebirds, our chirpy little friends who have welcomed us home so often with their hysterical screeching. I have asked my American-Cypriot friend, Galatia, if she will telephone the Ayios Neophytos monastery and find out if the monk in charge of the birds would like ours to add to his collection. He has a large cheerful aviary in the cloister garden where his birds have plenty of space to fly.

Thursday

Galatia reports back that Father Lucas is happy to take the parrots. He suggests we telephone before coming so that all will be ready to receive them.

Saturday

I have managed to sell the old Rover. I have not told Tim that the buyer is a flashy Nicosia businessman, sporting a gold neck chain and many signet rings. He wants it, he says, not for personal use but for display, mounted on the pavement in front of his oriental carpets emporium. Once the property of a respected Turkish diplomat, the old car has come down in the world at last.

Tuesday

Dearest Ma

Oh, the sadness of having to leave this place! A large stone
sits on my chest and hampers my breathing. Tim's arm is
making poor progress. The nerves were badly bruised by the
tight plaster and he is spending a good deal of each day at
the Rehab Clinic. We are fortunate he can stay so close by,
with his parents. But he has missed the Law Conference! I
went to Nicosia to attend several of the sessions including
one on Human Rights. However, I found it difficult to take
in the gist of much that was said, as the irony of our situation
seemed to dampen my pleasure and interest. Tim had given
so much of himself to the creation of the Conference.

I will write more later.

All love

Libby

Sunday

Crystalla returns to New York tonight. Her visit has brought great
joy to Old Kemon and Maria. I went with her to attend her last
service, a morning one at the new little chapel of Ayios Raphael
down below the village. A new tarmac road has replaced the old
dirt road, which continues on its dusty way below the chapel.
The little building has been built with immaculate care, its creamy
stone walls, polished marble floor and timber-vaulted ceiling
topped with a tiled roof; I recall the months of toil the builders
endured during last summer's heatwave, Father S doing his bit as
well. Fresh new icons decorate the iconostasis. Indoors, many of
us had to stand in the tiny space. One young boy remained firmly
rooted to his chair as several elderly ladies entered. No one

247

suggested to him that he do otherwise, and the ladies stood!

Outside the chapel a row of ugly overalls hung on coathangers. Beside them a new notice reads.

The females should be modestly dressed with a shirt until the knee and not with sleeveless dresses.
It is forbidden for the females to wear trousers.
It is forbidden also the lipstick.
Men must wear trousers and not sleeveless T-shirts.

This notice sets a sterner tone than the one outside Ayios Maria: *You are requested to dress in modesty when entering in the church.*

Both reflect the changing times, recognized by all bar the Church. I suspect that the bit about the lipstick is directed at the likes of me.

Our priest is doing his best to get the road past the new church closed. This idea is being strongly resisted by the villagers, who use it to visit their farms.

Friday

About seven thousand people, old and young, Greek Cypriot and Turkish Cypriot, attended a festival in the UN buffer zone in Nicosia this week. It was called The Festival of Mutual Understanding. Seven Greek and Turkish Cypriot political parties organized the event under the unlikely auspices of the Slovak Ambassador.

'Dear friends,' said Ambassador Rozbora. 'Dear Cypriots. You have brought to this Festival your open minds and hearts to meet and talk to your former co-villagers and personal friends from the other side, whom you cannot meet whenever you please. It is my strong belief that you will take back to your homes a wish to be together again and make all Cypriots one undivided family.'

However, the Occupied North 'foreign ministry' announced shortly before the festival that the Turkish Cypriots could not cross the checkpoint without identity cards. This included children. Many families who did not possess cards for their children were kept waiting so long at the checkpoint that they turned back.

At the street party, young people drank and talked together, some swapping photos of each other's 'lost houses'. An elderly man from the Greek Cypriot side searched for his Turkish friend. But time has moved on. He learned that his friend was dead, and handed the man's family a ten-pound note in order that prayers may be said.

Tuesday

The parrots have gone! The house seems so silent. The only chatter now comes from the swallows, who have not nested here this year but still swoop in and out as if searching for old memories. The incident with the third swallow (a bossy maiden aunt?) who destroyed last year's nest has not been forgotten, alas.

The monastery gave us a warm welcome today. Early this morning Nicos helped me with the tricky job of removing five nest boxes from the aviary. Last night, I crawled into the aviary and placed handkerchief tissues in the nest box openings, but not so tightly wedged as to prevent the flow of oxygen. How surprised I was to be woken as usual by Pyramus' dawn chorus! He had removed the paper tissue and he and his wife were back on their favourite perch. I crawled into the aviary on all fours, there being little room to stand, and managed to secure Thisbe in my butterfly net. She allowed herself to be returned to her box without fuss. Pyramus was another matter. Spotting a crack in the aviary door which I had failed to secure properly from my cramped position, he darted out and circled the courtyard, landing at length in the gardenia bush. A game of hide-and-seek followed. At last, perhaps with the thought that life without Thisbe would be intolerable, he allowed me to lower the net over his small pulsating body and return him to his wife.

Galatia arrived about 7.30 and we set off for the other side of the island.

The black-robed figures of Father Lucas and Father Pararetos greeted us on our arrival. We were led down the steps into the monastery garden, nest boxes clutched under our armpits. I had hoped that our family would be placed in the larger aviary but was dismayed when we were shown a much smaller one nearby, by no means up to the five-star accommodation back home. However, thankful that our little friends would get plenty of tender loving care from the kindly Father Lucas, I allowed him the privilege of introducing them to the two residents. These were a pair of masked-faced African parrots, very similar to ours but wearing the distinctive black rings around their eyes which have given them their name. Ours are the peach-faced variety. Pinky, introduced first, fluttered to a convenient perch and sat there, looking dazed, while one by one the others were released and began to career about her. Pyramus and Thisbe made straight for the perch on which the two resident birds snuggled together in anxious communion. I hope that Pyramus won't get too bossy, but it does not look hopeful.

After the settling in process was complete and photographs were taken of birds and humans alike, Father Lucas enquired if we could care for some breakfast. Accepting his offer gladly, we were led to the refectory, where a long table, stretching the length of the room, was laid with some thirty settings. The monks themselves having already eaten, Galatia and I sat in solitary state to tuck into a delicious repast of oranges, sliced tomatoes, olives and cucumbers, toast and coffee.

Back home it is lonely. No Tim and no parrots! I feel I have betrayed our feathered friends, their new home is so small and narrow. I hope they will forgive me.

Wednesday

I drove down today to the coast to bid farewell to Old Crystalla, who spends much of her time now with Maroulla and husband. She wept and pressed my hand to her cheek. I was plied with food but had no appetite. Maroulla tells me that her mother's heart is not good, but that they will be back for our Easter celebrations. Old Demetri is as spry as ever, and so is Madonna. I paid the latter a visit this afternoon. She made short work of the six carrots I had bought from the greengrocer's van. I gave her a final brushing and left the curry comb on a fence post, in the unlikely event that it will be taken up again.

Monday

The house has been stripped bare, bare to its bones. The front parlour, once bright with our Indian and Persian hangings, the comfortable blue armchair, the yellow daisies (plastic but not so you would know it) in their ceramic pot, is now reduced to the unrelenting little settee with the iron legs. The photograph of the Pope and the carved looking glass are gone. All that remain on the walls are Thekla's icons of St George slaying his dragon and a host of assorted saints. Perhaps, before long, St George will be slaying our ghosts as well.

The sitting room is bare also, bar the three orange chairs. It looks as clinical as the day Melanie gave it such a scrubbing, hurling her buckets of water about, paddling to and fro in her bare feet. Maria has taken the off-cut of carpet we bought together in Larnaca. It is for her brother, who has brought his family back from the troubles in Colombia. He must now try to make a fresh start here.

The kindly Takis of the Rest Place has helped me sell some of our furniture. The pair of us set off last Wednesday in his utility truck, the Indonesian bookcase rearing above the other goods in much the same manner as did Thekla's cabinet in Tassos' truck three years ago. In like manner it also had an altercation with an inaminate object, this time the branch of a tree. The incident failed to do more damage than leave a number of scratches on the woodwork, and I found myself hardly bothered that the value of the piece would now be somewhat reduced. I am cultivating an air of indifference I do not feel.

'Don't worry,' I reassured the apologetic Takis. 'It is nothing.'

On the way down the mountain Takis began to talk about his brother. With every Cypriot, these things are painfully close to the surface still. Sooner or later they crop up in conversation. Takis' brother is one of 'The Disappeared'. He was a carpenter. When the invasion by Turkey began, the brother, a father of five children and with a pregnant wife, was sent off to Kyrenia with a gun. He has not been seen since. The government gave his family a little money. Not much.

'Makarios, he is no good,' Takis assures me as we rattle coastward. 'He wants British out of Cyprus. They go and the Turks come! These churchy churchy people! They should go back to church, not mix with politics!'

Upstairs today, the view from the roof terrace is shrouded in cloud as welcome rain sweeps across the island from the west. All night the thunder grumbled across the mountains. The bougainvillaea droops beneath the deluge and small rapids hurry down the lane. The hanging chimney in the spare bedroom sends merry drips into the green bucket, but the heirloom wardrobe is dry enough.

Nicos came before the rain to remove our green mesh 'sun roof'. He assures me it will be useful for his doves. Next to his old mother, the doves come high in his affections. They occupy a series of unsightly home-made cages which stand at the entrance to his house, a new 'annexe' being added each time Nicos acquires a few more birds. The doves seem happy enough with their somewhat cramped quarters, and their billing and cooing can be heard from down the lane. Our green mesh will provide a smartening effect as well as a shield against the worst of the sun.

252

I offered our three air conditioners to Thekla but she was not interested. A pity, as a young English scuba-diver from Ayia Napa bought them at a knock-down price!

Monday

I watched helplessly on Sunday as Peter tore the smart green mesh from its supports. Rip! Rip! Rip! One rip for each year! That structure represented my most superior do-it-yourself craftsmanship; hours of love and careful work went into its construction. Now, all is gone in less than a minute!

The courtyard, too, is swept clean of our pots and shrubs. A South African Cypriot, returned home from his adopted country and its uncertain future, has bought the bulk of our pots. He brought a moonlighting Kurd with him, a poor hungry-looking fellow whom he ordered about as he once did his black employees.

'Here, you! Put that one on the truck first. No. Not *that* one! Here. *This* one. Watch what you're doing, you'll break the lot' etc.

The Kurd said nothing, but worked with a will, glad no doubt to have a job, even a boss such as this one. The conditions in his own country must make any life a paradise in comparison, though I was sorely tempted to remind his boss that he isn't in South Africa now.

Evagora has taken the Norfolk Island pine and the grevillea. Pots of geraniums, the mauve bougainvillaea and the camellia have gone to Chrisso, the mukhtar's wife, Myafora and Androulla, together with the prized portulaca. Koulla has taken the gardenia bush. She brought her hefty son to help lift its pot, but it broke and he nicked his thumb (a very small nick) on her old spade. Koulla was left to stagger off with the precious soil, re-ladled into a kerosine tin, while her son followed, nursing his thumb and the empty pot.

Our neighbour-of-the-barking-dogs remained. In a last gesture, a peace-offering at the end of our somewhat fragile relationship, I offered to buy some of her lace. I have to admit it is beautifully worked! This thought soothes me when I consider how grossly I was overcharged.

Tuesday

Easter has been easier on our village priest this year, due to the fact that the onset of the hot weather has been delayed by storms and rain. After the Epitaphios Procession through the village on Easter Saturday night, it is his final duty to go through the village blessing each house. This is an onerous task at the end of the protracted Easter proceedings, but Easter Saturday was pleasantly cool and the air fresh from rain. I attended the Midnight Service, the church as crowded as always and I was thankful to have found a seat. I sat next to Old Crystalla and Androulla, one of whose sons acts as an assistant to Father S at some of the services. The husbands of these ladies were seated towards the front. We passed our lighted candles from one to another, and while the fireworks popped outside and the bonfire roared, we greeted each other with '*Christos anesti, Alithinos anesti*' as before. I felt too shy to ask Father S if he would bless our house. I am 'not Orthodox' and besides, I remind myself, it will not be our house for much longer.

Looking out from our bedroom window when all was over and the village quiet once more, I noticed that someone had not had time to bring in Old Crystalla's washing. A pair of trousers hung on the line and some socks. It has been a busy day.

MAY

Friday

It has been difficult to write. My chief solace these early summer days is the little bay where I swim each morning and then the climb to the cliff top to sit in the shade in Costas' garden. Here the willowy gums cast their patchy shade and today there were swallows! Half a dozen of them were swooping and turning over the little taverna and in and out among the delicate acacias.

Costas was watering his garden when I arrived early this morning.

'You are a very sexy lady,' he assured me as I stood before him in my battered straw hat and faded sarong.

'Thank you, Costas. I could do with that.'

With a giant-sized hose, more appropriate for fire fighting than for gardening, Costas was drenching his bright green lawn and the surrounding shrubs, the force of the jet stream truly impressive in this drought-stricken land.

'Where do you get all this water? Have you a spring?'

'From the government,' he replied enigmatically. 'The water, it is no good for drinking but it is very good for the plants.'

So saying, he sent an avalanche of the stuff on to a flower bed, all but uprooting a bed of small shrubs which have soft, feathery leaves. They lay flattened in the red mud.

After my swim, I went up the path to the taverna.

'*Kalimera*, Elizabeth!' Old Panayiotis came hurrying forth, patting me on the cheek as usual as if I were a two-year-old. 'Cyprus coffee?'

'*Para kalo*, Panayiotis. One sugar only. *Meteo.*'

With a nod Panayiotis shuffles towards the kitchen and I know, as usual, he will not let me pay for it.

'Tomorrow. *Avrio*. You pay *avrio.*'

'But you'll never make any money if you don't charge! Then you and your family will starve!'

'You are my friend. You pay tomorrow.'

I linger in this little oasis for as long as possible, loath to leave. Its kindliness envelops me like a cloak. The world beyond, out there over the bay and to the far lands yonder, can crash about as much as it likes. I gaze at Costas' flower beds, the flattened plants reviving a little and beginning to sit up after their pummelling. In their aviary Costas' budgerigars chirrup away. The swallows dive to catch the straying insect. The hot air hums. Beyond the garden the land looks more and more moon-like in the drought. Winter rains have been sparse down here. The olives are more grey than blue under their dressing of powdery dust. Not a flicker of air moves the thin drooping leaves of the eucalypts, which stand mute and pale. Along the highways the hardy oleanders will soldier on.

I do not tell Panayiotis that maybe I cannot come for his coffee tomorrow. There is so much to do still and so little time. Last week I drove down to Larnaca and bought myself a new umbrella. It will be raining in England.

Postscript

Mary, the author's friend from Australia, was able to visit her home village in Northern Cyprus when she paid a return visit to the island in October 2003. Border restrictions between the two halves of the island have now been eased.

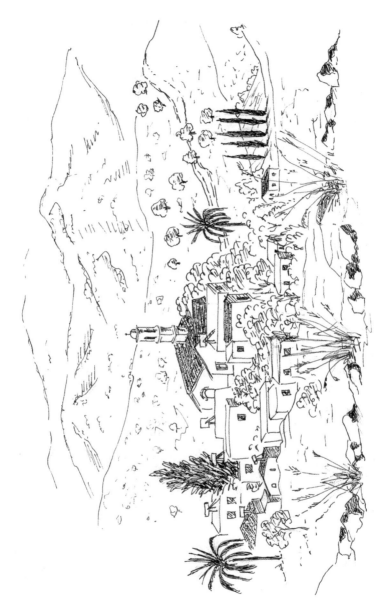

259

GLOSSARY

avrio	=	tomorrow
efharisto	=	thanks
ella	=	come
endaxi	=	OK
kalimera	=	good morning
kalinichta	=	good night
kalispera	=	good afternoon
kato	=	less
kleftiko	=	lamb simmered in foil
limoni	=	lemon
lokmades	=	doughnuts
lookoomathes	=	ditto
meteo	=	medium
mukhtar	=	mayor or head man
ne	=	yes
oxi	=	no
pano	=	more
para kalo	=	please
poly kala	=	very good
poly zesty	=	very hot
spiti	=	house
stifado	=	beef or rabbit goulash
sto kalo	=	go well
tavas	=	meat and rice dish
thelo isihia!	=	I want quiet!
yia sas	=	hello